TEAMBUILDING

A N D

TOTAL QUALITY

TEAMBUILDING

A N D

TOTAL QUALITY

A GUIDEBOOK TO TQM SUCCESS

*How to organize, gain commitment, build
teamwork, and use Quality Management tools
to strengthen your business*

Gene H. Milas

Engineering & Management Press

Printed in the United States of America.

| 00 | 99 | 98 | 97 | 1 | 2 | 3 | 4 | 5 |

Library Of Congress **Cataloguing–In–Publications Data**

Milas, Gene H., 1939–
    Teambuilding and total quality : a guidebook to TQM success/ by Gene H. Milas.
      p. cm.
    Includes index.
ISBN: 0898061733
1. Teams in the workplace. 2. Total quality management. I. Milas, Gene II. Title

HD66 .M54 1997   97-13900

ENGINEERING & MANAGEMENT PRESS
25 Technology Park/Atlanta, Norcross, GA 30092
Phone 770-449-0461 Fax: 770-263-8532

                        Director: Eric Torrey
                        Editor: Forsyth Alexander
                        Designer: Candace J. Magee
                        Publishing Assistant: Matthew Orsagh

Printed by McNaughton & Gunn.

Contents

Preface

THIS SECTION OF *Teambuilding and Total Quality* has been written to provide an expedient means of evaluating how suitable this material is to your business situation. In short, will this book give you fair value for your expenditure, and, of far more importance, can it help your business?

In the practice of quality, as in politics, there are both liberal and conservative views. The liberal, or more social, view generally holds that a motivated individual can, as part of a motivated team, provide the majority of the impetus needed to make TQM succeed. In this view, the emphasis is on humanistic skills, rather than those obtained through technical training. The opposing or conservative view, on the other hand, holds that training, management, and engineering tools and techniques are the keys to success in the world of quality and productivity improvement.

Teambuilding and Total Quality has been written to fill a void in the volumes of published materials on total quality management. TQM books that exist today seem to fall into two distinct sectors, presumably based primarily on the backgrounds and experiences of the authors. As described above, the conservative author champions the use of statistical techniques as weapons to fight real and perceived declines in quality and productivity. Statistical process control (SPC), in concert with work team formation and training, is frequently presented as an off-the-shelf packaged approach to curing business problems. Many times this approach to improvement quotes the successes of Deming, Juran, Crosby, and other quality management notables.

A second, and now perhaps more popular approach, envisions the widespread use of teams, teamwork, employee empowerment, and worker self-direction. Advice of this nature is frequently published by academic professionals, human resource consultants, and those that generally have humanities backgrounds. Here, the emphases are on "people-" rather than "thing-" related concepts. In this approach, the application of scientific problem-solving and some statistical techniques are secondary in importance to organizing, motivating, and empowering work groups.

In my view, success in TQM requires approximately equal portions of science and art, mixed according to the organization's goals and appetites for improvement. Early on, emphasis must be placed on establishing the vision (mission) for a TQM initiative, with dedication and commitment flowing from the absolute top of the organization. As goals and objectives are defined, and as employees become comfortable and establish trust in each other and the goals of the firm, training in work-group relationships and use of technical problem-solving approaches is appropriate. In and of themselves, training and teamwork are not panaceas. Success will result only when management shows unfailing commitment to the process of continuous improvement and to the recognition of even small victories. TQM is like a diet program designed to prolong the life of a seriously ill person. That person must make a commitment to follow the diet "forever," or suffer a serious consequence. In this analogy, the life of a business without commitment to total quality is possible, but sooner or later, it simply won't be competitive and will cease to exist.

Throughout this book I've used the term "visionary." In my view, the executive, manager, or company owner who undertakes a total quality vision must truly see the potential not seen by others, and undertake a *crusade* to spread the practice of TQM. I've also preferred to use the term initiative when speaking about Total Quality, since I feel personally uncomfortable with the term *program.*

The materials in this commentary are based on fact; all planning, organizing, and procedural details in the pages following are based on successful installations of quality initiatives in industry. This is not an "overview" of TQM, but a real, planned, engineered, orchestrated, "how-to-do-it" book. The sequence of events has been tested in practice and found to be successful. The practices and procedures detailed in the book are taken from real companies that have implemented TQ and teambuilding initiatives over the past several years. With that said, however, be cautioned that this is not a "cookbook"; where mistakes have or can be made, they are identified and discussed.

Further, the material has been developed in the course of a multi-faceted professional and business career. My background includes management in high technology businesses, college-level teaching, marketing and presentation of technical training seminars, and engineering and management consulting. My engineering education, a graduate business degree, and substantial management and consulting experience have given me a succinct and objective view of the world of TQM and teambuilding. I believe I can rationally balance the advantages and uses of statistical tools and the more humanistic theories of worker motivation.

Finally, this work addresses what is perhaps the most important, but least used business fact. The employee, not the initiative, the tools, or the work group, is the key to continuous improvement of operations within the business. The employee is the source of first-hand knowledge about the manufacturing process. He or she is the tool for forming effective work groups, and the vehicle for insuring the continued prosperity of the enterprise. The employee's reaction to the implementation of TQM is a response that must be nurtured with appropriate leadership, facilitation, recognition, and rewards.

Today, TQM fundamentals do not differ essentially from productivity enhancement strategies of the decades between 1930 and the 1950s, nor are they much improved. Then, a fashionable theme was "Work smarter... not harder." The tools of a program known as work simplification were enlisted to direct manufacturing workers toward applying their job knowledge to solve problems. What is different is management's realization that boundless quality and productivity improvements lie within the minds of employees. These riches can be harvested for the common good through commitment, trust, and teamwork.

Dedication

For Juli.

TEAMBUILDING

A N D

TOTAL QUALITY

CHAPTER 1

STOP TALKING AND START DOING

"We never got much out of our TQM program.
But then, we never put much into it, either."

– AN ANONYMOUS MANAGER

The quotation above could probably be attributed to scores of otherwise enlightened and progressive managers and executives across the United States and around the world. In the past decade, American business has been searching for a tool, technique, idea, or paradigm that would return it to the vital, competitive, growing, and rewarding entity it was in the post-World War II years. The once-proud business behemoth of the free world seems to have become a second-class citizen. Certainly, the US can supply quantity. Quality, however, has rapidly become another question.

The Rebirth of Value

CONSUMERS WANT VALUE in products and services. Value, by definition, provides the functions required at the lowest cost; value can be increased by lowering cost, increasing functionality, or both. The consumer of the last decade has come to equate value with obtaining and owning a product or using a service. The many factors influencing value are appropriateness to the task intended, initial quality, long-term serviceability and reliability, salvageability, technical support, warranty, and many other intrinsic and extrinsic factors. In all cases, the informed consumer makes a judgment of value relative to the many suppliers of a given product or service. Further, an important determinant in all characteristics is perception of value.

Value has many dimensions, but it has become clear that today's consumer includes quality in all definitions and forms of value. When competing products are available in abundance, the consumer cannot afford to ignore a calculation of value, however brief, when making a purchasing decision. In general, the consumer compares relative value in proportion to the cost of the product. The head of a household will spend little time shopping for milk or bread. He or she will devote substantially more time to a major appliance or vehicle purchase.

There is one qualified exception, and it has crippled American industry from the 1970s to the present day: the consumer will remember experiences with poor quality, and avoid those products in the future. This truism applies to any purchase decision.

A New Concept

THERE HAVE BEEN QUALITY "SOLUTIONS" in the past, among them statistical quality control, "total" quality control, SPC, and others. These essentially were new presentations of accepted quality engineering tools, for use by the quality and technical professionals in the business organization.

Rather than being simply a new method, tool, or procedure, total quality management is a new concept. Total quality presents several new ideas and demands a number of new responses.

The customer is the focus. This includes both external and internal customers and extends beyond the company's walls to its vendors and suppliers. Each member of the team must address quality and productivity issues throughout the overall value-adding process.

Commitment is absolute. It must start at the top and permeate the organization. Although a TQ initiative may start with a few visionary executives, the total commitment of all organization employees must be pursued. TQM is not a tactic, but a long-term and forever business strategy. As such, it becomes one of the values and principles that are the life's blood of any firm.

Management is responsible for success or failure of TQ. Much of the knowledge needed to improve a process resides in the workforce and with the internal and external customer; only management, however, can make changes happen. Furthermore, responsibility for establishing and improving processes lies with management, as does the quality of supplier products and services received.

A "quality policy" is imperative. A clear and concise policy on quality is important and necessary for focusing company resources. At the top, the quality policy is the mission statement and its ancillary values, which define the overriding long-term operating principles. At lower levels, the organization needs to understand that "business as usual" philosophies are no longer acceptable, and that there are specific quality goals associated with every operation. In every case, error-free product or service is the target.

Everyone is a quality manager. The organization should avoid appointing a "TQM Director," "Quality and Productivity Manager," and the like. Large organizations should also avoid using "Vice-President of Corporate Quality," or similar names. In the TQM initiative, every individual and every team will be given the resources of a quality inspector and manager. It is an error to perceive that one department, executive, or manager in the organization is the apex of quality planning and implementation. Managers, directors, and executives could be given more appropriate titles, such as "Quality Team Coordinator," "Customer Service Manager," "Quality Council Administrator," and so forth. In summary, all employees must understand, practice, and work toward accomplishing the mission.

Teamwork is mandatory. Teams provide the venue for extracting the creative and innovative ideas from each worker. Teamwork encourages communication, rewards accomplishment, and creates new enthusiasm in the organization.

Teams must be trained in TQM and quality management concepts, and in the use of specific tools for creative quality and productivity improvement. Since everyone in the organization will be part of a team, everyone must be trained. The company must focus training resources on those tools and techniques that will accomplish the mission and support the firm's objectives. Training is also important for measuring progress and must eventually be used to measure the success of the new initiative. Many companies structure training plans as if they were strategic business plans, determining the topics and duration of training for each employee group over a number of years. Training commitments per employee may be in the range of 40 to 120 hours annually.

Follow-through is important. TQM is not a "program of the day" that will disappear within a few business cycles. It is important to promote the entire staff's proficiency in teambuilding and other tools and techniques.

Improvement is infinite. By definition, TQ focuses on continuous improvement. The organization cannot put an end date or fiscal or business calendar milestones on the activity. Analogous to a serious medical problem, the treatment for survival and business growth demands a lifetime commitment to change. Certainly, the TQ initiative may change in nature; people and their responsibilities may change, the name, theme, and operating model may change, and assuredly customers and their wants and needs will change. The absolute focus of everyone in the organization, however, cannot change. Continuous improvement must be intrinsic to operating the business.

A nurturing and rewarding work environment is necessary if company goals are to be attained within a formal and structured process improvement plan. People must be appropriately and genuinely recognized for their accomplishments.

Starting the Initiative

THERE ARE TWO MAJOR APPROACHES to implementing a Total Quality plan in any organization; they have sometimes been called the "technical approach" and the "management approach." The technical approach advocates using specific technical or engineering–oriented tools, resources, and techniques to solve the problems of manufacturing or business operations. The use of tools is oriented to production processes and the stabilization and control of process variability. Clearly, this approach is intended for those comfortable with scientific tools–namely, engineering and technical personnel.

Using management skills to enter the TQM arena is another approach. Nominally, these include teambuilding, leadership, conflict resolution, communication, and group dynamics. While this approach provides the humanistic values necessary for melding a cooperative, dynamic organization, it may fall well short of the technical expertise needed to address production problems.

The answer lies somewhere between the two. TQM teams must have, or be provided with, the skills to deal effectively in two scenarios. First, they must work together and communicate positively; second, they must solve the current problem with whatever technical approach is appropriate. Each organization must assess its staff's capabilities in both technical problem-solving and human relations areas.

Before proceeding on the road to total quality, visionary executives or managers must benchmark the existing abilities of their employees. It is usually appropriate to engage outside assistance for this activity, and perhaps for the duration of the entire initiative.

An organization must not purchase an "off-the-shelf" program to implement TQ. The issues, variables, and variations between and among businesses create unique factors for each enterprise. These must be assessed and dealt with differently. Further, of the many "packaged" quality programs available today, none are totally adequate without some degree of customization. In general, pre-packaged statistical process control programs are the most likely tools and techniques to be commercially purchased as a stand-alone product. Even in this case, the company should select (presumably with the advice of a professional in the field) a package that addresses the specific, identified training needs of its program. Also, significant attention must be paid to the method of training delivery. It may not be appropriate, for example, to utilize computer-interactive training in a work environment with little computer literacy. In this case, platform presentations and "live" facilitation may be what is needed.

The visionary executive must survey needs, solicit proposals from selected quality and human resources professionals, and evaluate the respective approaches to TQ implementation. He or she should examine each competing approach to assure a blend of techniques. The proposals should provide a time-phased schedule, sources for all training expertise and materials, and examples of successful installations (including references). Any and all sources must emphasize a steady, consistent, well-planned process, that identifies key milestones and dates. All should address formulation of the Mission and supporting values and principles early in the proposed plan.

Some Key Questions

A FEW KEY QUESTIONS THAT SHOULD be addressed before proceeding are listed here. Unfortunately, there are no "road maps" to TQ success. There are simply cautions and some directions based on experience. In general, the successful initiative will have answered the following:

- Will this initiative tie to real business or competitive challenges for the organization? The goals and strategy of the business must be disclosed fully and honestly to all members of the team. Further, the Cost of Quality must be defined.
- Will the organization's existing culture support TQ? If not, specific training and human resources actions may be necessary to prevent "instant roadblocks."
- Are the existing communications channels consistent, clear, and timely? Everyone in the organization must have access to information in a prompt, accurate, and unbiased manner. Communication practices may need some fine tuning, particularly if the organization's history of labor/ management relations has been less than successful.
- Does everyone understand what total quality is and what continuous improvement means? Some education may be necessarybefore a formal kickoff.
- Is there an appreciation for the benefits of teamwork? If employees tend to be individual rather than team players, actions that enlighten the workforce may be necessary.
- What's in it for us? Management must answer this final question satisfactorily. While there are a number of verbal answers to be given, the best answer is, "Results." These come from commitment, planning, and timely execution of logical steps in the TQ plan.

When the questions are answered and the resources selected, it is then time to address a specific plan, organize resources, and formulate the mission.

CHAPTER 2

All About Quality

"Consumers are statistics. Customers are People."

– Stanley Marcus

There are many definitions of quality, including conformance to specifications, conformance to or exceeding customer expectations, customer satisfaction, or simply delighting the customer at every turn. These all necessitate focusing on the customer's needs while monitoring competition.

The following are among the myriad definitions of quality:

- *Conformance to the customer's requirements.* This is generally considered an excellent definition when the requirements are known. Few customers know their needs completely. Quality is like shopping for a piece of art or an antique; frequently, the buying decision and the happiness with the purchase are based on "love at first sight."
- *Fitness for use by the consumer.* Presumably, this means that the product or service is safe, workable, attractive, functional, and meets at least the minimum needs of the potential customer.
- *Meeting or exceeding customer expectations.* Many would argue that "exceeding customer expectations" is the very essence of TQM. This, of course, implies that all fundamental specifications

are met first, and that the customer is delighted by bonus features, price concessions, or other functionalities.

• *Customer satisfaction.* This is perhaps the most nebulous, and yet the most engrossing and encompassing definition. If there is acceptance of total customer focus in the mission statement, then this is probably the most workable definition.

• *Meeting product specifications.* Simply, this is delivering what is advertised, no more and no less.

It may be useful to think of quality as a product or service attribute with two distinct sets of requirements. These are how well the physical specifications defined for the product are met and how the customer views your accomplishment. Some critical factors include your price versus the competition's, prompt deliveries, and after-the-sale service.

In sum, the quality of a product or service may be defined in any manner acceptable to the two parties involved in a business transaction. They are, simply, the company and the customer. When the customer is satisfied and when the company has accrued enough revenue to pay expenses and turn a profit, the enterprise is considered successful, and the relationship continues. The key to survival is assurance that customers perceive a continuing value from the relationship. Value is the absolute worth of an item when compared to the price paid; value is increased by decreasing price, increasing function, or a combination of both. If other suppliers consistently provide more value to the customer, successes will be short-lived.

Characteristics of Quality

MANY SAY THEY "KNOW QUALITY when they see it." This is an accurate statement. The following are the factors they are seeking:

• *service-life or duration factors.* Also called time factors, these include maintainability, serviceability, reliability, and endurance. For most products, guarantee that the product will function properly has a substantial influence on salability;

• *intrinsic factors.* These may include honesty, integrity, fairness, ethics, and customer service provided to or perceived by the user;

- *aesthetics.* These include perceived beauty, color, taste, and a host of other semi-tangible parameters; and
- *physical factors.* These include structural strength, weight, height, density, volume, finish, and other items.

These factors are said to characterize quality.

Total Quality Management

THE TQM PROCESS HAS MANY DEFINITIONS because of its nebulous origins. Unlike a copyrighted procedure or proprietary process, there is no "birth date" for TQM. Its beginnings were effected by the confluence of two cultures (Japan and the U.S.), the U.S. government (Department of Defense), and several authorities in the field (Shewart, Ishikawa, Deming, Juran, Crosby, et al.). It is generally agreed, however, that TQC/TQM is a post-World War II innovation.

In the United States, early TQM-type programs were called zero defects (ZD) and total quality control (TQC) programs. The TQC approach targeted all working processes in a firm. Managerial and statistical techniques were used to measure and control quality. As more industries necessarily became involved with continuous improvement initiatives, the name and procedures evolved to a management concept.

Unfortunately, the total quality movement foundered for a number of years. Then, declining shares of American goods and services in world markets and perturbations in the US economy created a renewed emphasis on quality and productivity. This provided new incentives for revisiting the issues of quality, productivity, and the creative contributions of employees. Today, a commitment to TQM in some form is a necessity for every business owner and manager.

Although many definitions are available, the following description of TQM is succinct and effective: *"Total Quality Management is the continuous improvement of products, processes, and services through work activities which involve the entire organization in an integrated effort to satisfy the needs and expectations of the customer."*

TQM means transforming the way companies manage their businesses. Rather than focusing daily energies on small, recurring, and sometimes irrelevant problems, managers and employee teams extend their views to fundamental and critical work processes. By examining processes, or the "grand strategies" by which products and services flow throughout a company, the business can easily determine areas that need improvement. Furthermore, the use of appropriate problem-solving tools makes selecting and prioritizing areas a reasonably simple matter.

Genuine total quality improvements are always accompanied by productivity improvements. Such improvements affect net revenue and enterprise growth. Growth and success breed enhanced product salability, increased market share, reduced field failure rates, improved customer image, and long-term success.

The very nature of improvement can create initial apprehension about job security; increased productivity has, after all, historically displaced portions of the workforce in some industries. The visionary manager or executive must remain steadfast. Long-term commitment and success in TQM will yield growth in the labor market, not decline.

Continuous Improvement

CONTINUOUS IMPROVEMENT IS THE HEART of an ongoing and successful TQM initiative. Defined, continuous improvement is a program of planned actions that apply problem-solving tools and techniques to improve work processes and support the organization's mission.

The overall attitude of the business is key; is it devoted to an ongoing process of improvement or simply another short-term motivational program? The Japanese word for continuous improvement is kaizen, the orderly elimination of waste. This waste is not only material, but also labor, overhead, and any ineffective action that hinders production.

The philosophy of continuous improvement is simple. The business must have a long-term plan and organization-wide commitment to quality. Improvements in business and manufacturing operations are not sporadic. On the contrary, they are gradual. Individually taken, improvements may not be large, but the sum of successes over time is impressive.

Internal and External Customers

ANOTHER TQM FUNDAMENTAL IS THAT QUALITY products and services must be delivered to internal as well as external customers. The internal customer is anyone in the organization who receives an input of goods, information, data, or services from someone else in the organization. Essentially, each employee in a firm is a "mini-factory." His or her "product" is delivered to the next individual or group in the logical process that leads to shipping the product. In other words, each individual in the firm is a consumer of something, be it a report, a partially assembled product, an inspector's approval stamp, a verbal presentation, a lab analysis, or a test result. Everyone is both someone's customer and supplier. Thus, the entire enterprise is a complex, miniature economic model.

As an internal customer, each individual in the firm must eventually answer the question of how they perceive quality. Is it satisfaction? Meeting specifications? Delighting me? Exceeding demands? If the individual employee can truly appreciate the needs of the customer and his or her definition of quality, then engaging workforce energies in the TQM crusade becomes feasible.

Core Questions for the Workforce

ONCE AN ORGANIZATION APPRECIATES THE NEEDS of both internal and external customers, and commits to the principles of continuous improvement, the business and the visionary managers and executives may proceed. The next step is enlightening, training, and coaching employees and employee teams. At this point, an exact definition of quality may be meaningless; customer feedback, internal and external, will form the basis for actions. The actions will be centered on the basic processes of the business.

The following questions must be answered by every member of the team, at some point in the TQM process:

Are we meeting our current customers' requirements? As internal customers, are we satisfied with the quality of our many suppliers and their products?

11

Does our product or service offer true value to the point that our competitors' products are no longer being considered? If not, how do customers perceive "our" quality as opposed to "their" quality?

Have we created an environment that is challenging, rewarding, and self-perpetuating? True quality cannot coexist with a bored, dissatisfied, and disgruntled workforce.

Has everyone in the enterprise, and our suppliers, been offered an opportunity to join us in this endeavor? TQ successes should be propagated throughout the supply chain to maximize impact and assure the symbiotic growth of vendors and suppliers, as well as the principal business.

Are we proud of our achievements, and are we continually progressing? Continuous improvement should not be decelerated over time.

Once they understand the basics of quality and agree on some definitions, the visionary manager and his or her team must address the cost of quality, a key indicator of how successful the TQ plan will be in the future.

CHAPTER 3

The Cost of Quality

*"The chains of habit are too weak to be felt
until they are too strong to be broken."*

– Samuel Johnson

Almost a generation ago, Philip B. Crosby wrote *Quality is Free: The Art of Making Quality Certain.* This significant book is now an essential tool for quality professionals and business managers around the world.

Is quality free, however? There is no question that American businesses and industries have invested more resources per capita in quality and reliability issues than any other industrialized nation in the world. In one view, Crosby's contribution to the American economy has not been the recognition of assurance costs themselves, despite the title of his book. Instead, it is the development of a quality management system.

Quality has rapidly emerged as a new and distinctive discipline, with professional values, ethics, guidelines, and procedures. The quality professional today is no less unique and essential than a surgeon, an attorney, or a cleric. In fact, the growing and respected quality engineering field is rapidly developing into a separate management science. As the quality profession grows, so also do the concepts of quality systems and quality management.

As an evolving arena of management, quality initiatives are increasingly subjected to the controls, constraints, and measurements found in any business system. Quality is no longer personified by the old and wise gray-haired inspector at the end of the production line. It is a system, to be managed within cost and schedule constraints, along with the quality of the quality system itself.

The virtue of describing the cost of quality is that executives, when the true cost is appreciated, will develop a system to manage this parameter as they would any other. To perform the managing function, measures are necessary for tracking the impact of teambuilding and Total Quality Management. To achieve these measures, controls, constraints, and procedures must be put in place. This is all part of the process of acknowledging the substantial role and cost of producing quality products and services.

The cost of quality (COQ) is not the cost of running the quality department. Many modern managers have now accepted that; however, they still fail to realize that a finely tuned system that detects and computes COQ is a mandatory TQM requirement. To realize (and prove) the benefits of TQM, a company must have COQ data on a continuing basis, particularly during the effort's infancy. A primary goal of TQ should be benchmarking the current COQ for progress reports as the initiative advances. A truly successful initiative will show meaningful improvements in the COQ indicator, and those savings can be used to further teambuilding and TQM.

Quality Costs

IN THE PAST, QUALITY SYSTEMS typically included:
- engineering and inspection labor;
- gauge procurement and calibration;
- inspection tools;
- vendor quality assurance;
- instrumentation and metrology equipment; and
- a variety of in-house or contracted services.

These resources were used to compare product characteristics with the engineering specifications for those products. The cost of quality was found in the bottom-line actuals of the functional department's budget, be it Inspection, Quality Control, Product Assurance, or a host of other names.

Today, the management of quality and, consequently, the costs of quality are found in the operating budgets of many functional groups.

These typically include:
- the quality assurance and inspection departments;
- sales and marketing;
- design and manufacturing engineering;
- management staff departments;
- finance and accounting; and
- general and administrative overhead (sometimes called G&A).

General and executive managers have come to realize that the true cost of quality or *conformance* has many charges extraneous to the classic quality control function. Every defect or failure found by an inspector on the manufacturing floor has a definitive cost trail that affects multiple departments. A single quality-related transaction–a field failure and warranty reimbursement, for example–will typically affect every major discipline within the firm. A field failure in complex electronic gear may perturbate the following departments in a typical manufacturing firm. (This is a short list; a truly catastrophic product failure would cascade through many more disciplines in a large, multi-national firm.)

SALES OR MARKETING would have to interface with the customer to affirm the failure and provide disposition instructions and arrange for product replacement if applicable.

TRAFFIC would have to arrange for packaging and transporting the faulty equipment to a repair location, depot, or main manufacturing location. If the location is overseas, this department must also arrange for bonded warehouse, customs clearance, and tariff payment. If necessary, it would also have to provide packaging and shipping for replacement products.Finance or accounting would have to reimburse the customer for costs incurred under the warranty terms, adjust financial performance reports to reflect warranty and applicable refurbishment or rework costs, and adjust inventory and cost-of-goods-sold valuations for parts and accumulated direct labor.

QUALITY ENGINEERING would have to review and classify the defect, document it, provide instructions for corrective and remedial actions, and secure the equipment until repairs begin.

MANUFACTURING ENGINEERING would have to disposition equipment for repair, rework, or salvage.

MANUFACTURING would have to repair, rework, or salvage the equipment, as well as test it to re-certify acceptability.

INSPECTION would have to examine the equipment for conformance to original specifications. They then would have to affirm repairs, rework, or refurbishment as directed by the engineering staff..

PRODUCTION AND INVENTORY CONTROL would have to assure that existing part stocks and finished goods inventories are defect-free with regard to the problem in question.

PURCHASING would have to review the failure data to examine trends and assure conformance of the parts in the supplier pipeline.

DESIGN ENGINEERING would have to assist with repair and/or refurbishment disposition, review design specifications and provide design "fixes" if mandated, maintain history and traceable documentation for disposition and repair activities, and revise the product's bill of materials and specifications to reflect design improvements.

Cost of quality can be an enormous proportion of the bottom-line cost of doing business. Failures can no longer be simply "inspection problems," or "manufacturing problems." They certainly cannot be cured if management attends to only one discipline. Quality levels cannot be improved in the strategic long term simply by using more inspectors or conducting more frequent inspections; nor can they be improved by throwing money at manufacturing systems and controls.

Quality is a *system* that must be *managed*. Hence the term *quality management*.

In the past, traditional managers, when faced with tradeoffs between cost, schedule, and quality, almost always chose schedule and cost. As a result, many factory systems continue to be dedicated to controlling those parameters. Traditional belief was that it was more expensive to produce "good quality" than "bad quality," and that producing good quality created intolerable expenses. Today's visionary then finds that she or he has fewer mechanisms and reporting systems in place to track COQ than for any other plan or cost. It is in his or her best interest to establish a baseline COQ and the systems and guidelines that monitor it at the inception of the TQ process. In other words, tracking COQ should begin at the time the mission is formulated.

The Cost of Quality

COQ IS AN AGGREGATE MEASURE of all resources expended to assure, guarantee, correct, measure, and report the existence of acceptable quality in products. By definition, these costs include direct and indirect labor and materials and overhead, although measuring some costs accurately may be difficult.

The general definition of COQ consists of costs in five distinct groupings:

1. Internal failure costs–the costs due to defects found before the customer receives the product. By definition, any "touch up" or "fine tuning" beyond the basic first-pass should be considered an internal failure cost. Obviously, the earlier in the process a defect is caught, the less the cost penalty.

2. External failure costs–costs associated with defects found after the customer receives the product. As indicated earlier, this can be a significant factor, since it involves correcting and possibly retrieving the product from a remote location. Further, all first-pass factory costs that have been invested are now totally lost. Some managers group internal and external failures into a single classification, the cost of failure.

3. Appraisal costs–costs incurred to determine the degree of conformance. Essentially, these are the costs associated with the product assurance operations of quality control and inspection departments. These include inspecting and testing, as well as documenting. Appraisal also includes inspection of incoming supplier materials.

4. Prevention costs–costs of strategic and operations to minimize failure and apprasial costs. They may include design reviews, drafting product specifications and material requirements, producibility and manufacturability studies, training, test procedure development, product qualification testing, maintenance programs, and so forth.

5. Opportunity costs–lost revenues due to real or perceived quality programs. These are very real, yet they are difficult to assess. A prospective customer may decline a purchase for specific quality-related reasons.

The five cost groups can either, solely or in any combination, cause the following:

- *doing work over.* Anywhere in the business, clerical
or factory, salaried or hourly, the repetition of any work
event adds to COQ;

- *scrap.* A scrapped part, assembly, tool, procedure, report, or any unit of output penalizes the company not only for the cost of material, but also for any labor invested in disposition;
- *increased customer service.* Answering a complaint means added customer service labor. Failed products that are not returned also result in loss of labor, and may even create significant travel or telephone expenses;
- *inspection and testing.* Verifying or checking the completeness and accuracy of a prior event means additional testing and inspection expenses; and
- *logistics.* Innumerable and often intangible costs are associated with documentation, plans and schedules, purchases, inventories, accounting records, transportation, travel, insurance, training, and the many other effects created by product discrepancies. Conceivably, logistics could be the greatest single cost in a complex or high-technology company environment.

Measuring COQ

FEW EXECUTIVES, MANAGERS, OR EVEN TQ VISIONARIES are able to estimate accurately their firm's COQ without great energy and lengthy calculation. Almost invariably, the real COQ is greater than the best estimate or most careful calculation, simply because so many exogenous and intangible factors drive cost. High technology companies may spend literally millions of dollars doing work over. Most executives don't realize that sales revenue could be increased by perhaps 20 percent by simply paying more attention to the issues of rework and scrap.

What, then, is an acceptable or reasonable COQ? This is a question for which there are varied answers. Numerous surveys have been conducted in hopes of estimating COQ for various types of American businesses. The general consensus is that COQ can be as little as 5 percent or as high as 25 or 30 percent of sales.

COQ costs should be computed and measured in current year dollars and against one agreed-upon standard: sales revenue. In this manner, every employee, manager, executive, shareholder, and board member can tell instantly the company's growth potential when excesses are controlled.

Assuming there is demand for a company's product, and its price can be maintained or lowered in proportion to savings, the business's revenues can grow as a direct COQ function.

It may not be convenient for functional department heads to track dollars or relate to sales revenue, but it must be done somewhere. It would not be practical, for example, for one department to compute COQ against payroll and another to calculate it against purchased material dollars. To find the true impact of COQ, the various inputs (doing work over, customer service, scrap, and so on) must be computed at an action level, summarized to the highest level, and compared with that business's sales revenue. An analogy that impresses the staff with the importance of COQ might be helpful:

> *"One average field warranty claim costs about as much as an average*
> *three-bedroom house."*
> *"Replacing just one component after acceptance testing costs the equivalent*
> *of a compact automobile."*
> *"Every minute spent in downtime on the line for a reject buys a $300 suit."*

Most employees, even those with marginal appreciation for or knowledge of the problem, can understand the importance of quality and the COQ indicators when expressed in such terms.

Summary

IN SUMMARY, A VISIONARY EXECUTIVE and his or her staff should undertake assessing the true cost of quality as early as possible in the TQ initiative. A good place to start is with the more tangible records: rework, scrap, salvage, retesting, retrofits, warranty costs, direct labor, and other such accounted-for parameters.

Beyond that, recognize the hidden factory; it is where the bulk of COQ may exist. Look at customer service travel, phone calls, postage, "buy-back" products and reimbursements for freight and insurance, product replacements, square footage facility costs, capitalized inspection and test equipment, contract labor, vendor testing and penalty charges, good will and institutional advertising (particularly if done to overcome a quality problem in the marketplace), insurance claims, and other items.

In most companies, the aggregate magnitude of the cost of quality is phenomenal. Recognizing the components of COQ is a positive and necessary step toward becoming a TQ business.

ORGANIZING TEAM 1

*"There is nothing more difficult to take in hand,
more perilous to conduct, or more uncertain
in its success than to take the lead
in the introduction of a new order of things."*

– JEAN JACQUES ROUSSEAU

FOR TQ TO BE SUCCESSFUL in a business enterprise, that enterprise must first have a single individual with a vision of TQM. Vision is only a part of what is needed; executive authority to commit time and money also is important. Someone must be the catalyst, and preferably that someone should be a top executive.

No matter how committed he or she is, however, one person cannot do the TQM task alone. He or she must recruit a following for the cause. The sooner this can be done the better, since TQ involves a long-term management learning process.

A TQM initiative needs a steering committee composed of interested and committed members that espouse the visionary's goals and values. No executive can go far without assistance and cooperation; conversely, no group in the organization can direct change without the resources controlled by the visionary.

TEAM1 is a pseudonym for the steering committee that will serve as the visionary's "support group." A principal TEAM1 role is "cheerleading" for the executive, supporting the initiative in any way possible.

Another important TEAM1 function is to act as a "sounding board" in daily procedural issues. These issues involve organizing, planning, integrating systems, and handling the daily affairs of the continuous improvement initiative. The steering committee should be a model organization worthy of emulation.

TEAM1 is much like the president's cabinet. It is at once advisory, cautionary, agreeable, and, occasionally, stubborn. It functions as the visionary executive's eyes, ears, and conscience. TEAM1 has a vested interest in the success of its leader and the TQ process. There is no question that the visionary is the leader of the committee, but the process must be symbiotic and nurturing, not autocratic.

If the visionary is the general manager or plant manager, his or her staff reports may comprise the steering committee initially. It might also include representatives from human resources, accounting, legal, marketing, or other non-manufacturing (or non-value adding) departments. If the visionary is a corporate vice-president or executive, the steering committee may consist of that person's immediate staff, including plant or division managers, corporate HR staff, and manufacturing executives. Generally, the size of the steering committee should not be significantly larger than the leader's normal span of control.

When forming the steering committee, the visionary must clear a number of roadblocks. First and foremost, there will be the general attitude that this is another "program-of-the-year." The group must be constantly reminded that TQM is not such a program, and that it will progress beyond the current fiscal period. Second, innate workforce fears must be alleviated. Because the premise of TQM is to improve both quality and productivity, there may be some concern that work (and therefore jobs) may be eliminated. Employees will not "buy in" without substantial assurance of the initiative's objectives. Third, the installation may be doomed to failure by perceptions of the past, when indecision or poor decisions led to failure of other worthwhile tools, techniques, or training programs.

The importance of membership in the steering committee is sometimes reinforced by up-front training in team and group skills at the initiative's inception. A perceived lack of interest, motivation, response, or support from one or more staff members might be improved with timely intervention of an outside consultant or facilitator (more on this in later chapters).

The visionary executive should not assume that all training must take place at a level lower than the steering committee. TEAM1 cannot be separated from the rest of the company, nor can it be assumed that all TEAM1 members are sufficiently trained in the techniques of TQM and teambuilding.

Selecting TEAM1

TO A CERTAIN DEGREE, MEMBERS of the steering committee must be reflections of the visionary leader. The following are the characteristics that define ideal TEAM1 participants.

- *They must be an essential part of the business.* Each committee member must know the company, its history, people, policies, and procedures.
- *TEAM1 members must be communicators*–able to relate to the other team members and with the remaining parts of the organization.
- *They must believe that all people are innately creative* and skilled, and that employees can be entrepreneurial.
- *They must support training opportunities,* recognizing and taking actions to correct deficiencies.
- *They must be patient,* realizing that TQ paybacks require a long-term commitment.
- *They must believe that success and prosperity* are not possible unless their subordinates prosper and succeed.
- *Each TEAM1 member must also be open* to and recognize the need for training.

As the initiative matures, the leader may add representatives from various business departments or functions, bargaining units, and lower-level managers and supervisors. Permanent steering committee members need only be the visionary executive and a facilitator (internal or external).

Propagating the Vision

THE LEADER OF TEAM1 MUST IMPART his or her vision and enthusiasm to the group, then maintain interest and participation for the long haul. If the

TEAM1 leader can't motivate and rally his or her staff to the TQM call, then it's time to regroup, reorganize, and remind the staff of the source of their paychecks! When every committee member is dedicated to reaching the TQ vision and accomplishing the mission, then the visionary can turn the leadership reins over to others. To do this, the leader of TEAM1 must address, at a minimum, the following factors:

- **history and benefit.** Why have we, as an organization, come to this point? Why have we perceived the need for teambuilding and TQM? If we succeed, what are the rewards?;
- **objectives.** Informally, what are the "marching orders?" Where, exactly, do we want to go, and how are we going to get there?; and
- **organization.** How do we organize and attack the problem? Who's in charge, and for how long? How do we (I) fit into the master plan?

Steering Committee Roles and Responsibilities

THE STEERING COMMITTEE HAS THE AUTHORITY and responsibility to decide policy issues, approve the selection of pilot TQ areas and projects, and approve the use of resources, including employee time commitments. The committee also develops and approves plans, procedures, and schedules necessary for implementing the TQ initiative.

The committee members must document the operating procedures as they would any other business procedure.

Guidelines for TQM operating procedures are suggested below. Although any formal procedure will need to be customized for a particular company, these guidelines address the major topics that should be included in the document. The TQ steering committee must periodically and continually review the material for appropriate modifications, particularly in the areas of reward and recognition.

TQM Operating Procedure *(Suggested Outline)*

DOCUMENT PURPOSE AND SCOPE

APPLICABLE DOCUMENTS

DEFINITIONS AND GLOSSARY OF TERMS

OPERATING PROCEDURE

    Initiative Name, Theme, Logo, and Model

    Mission Statement, Guiding Principles and Values

    Steering Committee

        Composition

        Responsibilities

        Authority

    TQ Team Structure

        Team Leader Guidelines

        Team Member Guidelines

        Team Meeting Guidelines

        Team Operating Procedures

        Team Facilitator Guidelines

        Outside Consultant or Facilitator Role

RECOGNITION AND AWARD GUIDELINES

TRAINING CRITERIA, PROCEDURES, AND GUIDELINES

It is sometimes expedient for an outside consultant or facilitator to develop the TQM operating procedure outline. The infant steering group then can concentrate more fully on the tasks of organizing the initiative and less on the mechanics of trying to engineer consensus on a fairly lengthy document.

Additional steering committee functions typically include the following activities, grouped by phases of the initiative:

1. Start-up–
   - assessing readiness
   - defining a mission statement;
   - defining operating principles/values;
   - establishing an initiative theme or name;
   - establishing a model for initiative operation; and
   - setting initiative policies and procedures.

2. Operation and sustenance–
   - specifying team composition;
   - selecting specific implementation areas;
   - defining scope and constraints;
   - providing training;
   - providing support and protection from skepticism;
   - providing resources;
   - establishing and maintaining communications links;
   - nurturing change;
   - maintaining initiative momentum;
   - problem and roadblock avoidance;
   - developing a recognition/reward system;
   - providing funding and facilitating continuance
     of the initiative; and
   - providing internal and external publicity for
     the initiative.

Summary

TQM MUST HAVE A CHAMPION; the champion cannot be anyone other than an organization's senior executive. A solid steering committee composed of enthusiastic, committed members can help the senior executive "demystify" TQM so that it becomes a good and regular business practice. Otherwise it will become just another time-consuming, expensive, doomed-to-failure program du jour.

CHAPTER 5

THE MISSION

"For purposes of action nothing is more useful than narrowness of thought combined with energy of will."

– HENRI FREDERIC AMIEL

POOR ORGANIZATION AND PLANNING, followed by lack of commitment to common objectives will cause any management initiative to fail. When a company has no specific, long-term strategy or does not communicate strategic issues to employees systematically, the result is apathy. Apathy and ignorance breed well together; literally, ignorance means "I don't know," and apathy means "I don't care." These attitudes seem to prevail in companies that have autocratic structures or inspired leaders that are unable to communicate.

Establishing the business's goals and objectives up front is the core of good communication. This cannot be a reincarnation of a management by objectives program. The top executive and his or her staff must concentrate on condensing the company's strategic vision into a commonsense state-ment. This then becomes the company's mission.

Work Issues

FOR LACK OF A BETTER TERM, WORK ISSUES are those factors that have caused a company to want and need a new initiative. In short, what has happened that caused the organization to consider TQM? A sample listing might include:

- a dramatic loss of business or business opportunity caused by mis- or non-compliance with quality specifications;
- a catastrophic quality problem. The most tragic example of this is the Space Shuttle Challenger disaster of 1986;
- an insidious yet obvious decline in performance. This could include decreased process yields, increased field failures and warranty charges, rising customer complaints, or a combination of all or several;
- a steadily-increasing COQ;
- a general feeling that something bad is about to happen. Management is not quite sure what this might be, but intuition says to be wary;
- a new customer that strengthens business dramatically, but requires compliance with their supplier and vendor quality program structured around TQM. For example, such customers might be suppliers to the major US automobile manufacturers;
- a perceived need to adopt "state-of-the-art" management initiatives; and
- mounting employee dissatisfaction with current programs and policies (or lack thereof) and obvious organizational communication problems. This might be highlighted by laissez-faire employee behavior, high turnover rates, slowdowns, grievances, or even sabotage.

When the top manager has a valid perception of one or more of these conditions, and is personally committed to finding ways to improve, it is time to establish the organization's vision.

Vision and Mission

The words *vision* and *mission* are subjective, and their definitions can overlap somewhat. A company's vision is normally a long-term view. Founders, directors, and managers prescribe the firm's legacy. This vision can be a holistic, subjective summary of what is wanted for the firm. It is sometimes an inspirational statement.

A mission, on the other hand, is a more measurable statement of the enterprise's strategic goals. It conveys objectively the planned accomplishments for the TQM initiative in the short term.

The following are examples of visions versus missions:

Vision: To bring computer power to the people.

Mission: To become the market leader in home-based personal computing systems.

Vision: To serve the public, as nearly as we can, to its complete satisfaction.

Mission: To become the world's leading retailer of children's fashions.

Vision: To offer a catalog shopping experience comparable to none other.

Mission: To provide products that consistently conform to our customers' expectations of quality, price, delivery, and service.

The mission generally is used as a working tool. It more clearly focuses on measurable goals. The vision, while inspirational, is less of a business management tool and more of a public relations vehicle.

The Mission Statement

OTHER THAN COMMITMENT ITSELF, the mission statement is perhaps a firm's single most significant effort. The mission statement sets the tone for the TQM initiative. Everyone must think about their goals and the goals of the company. Further, it improves communications among those senior managers that will eventually lead the initiative as the TQM steering committee.

It is also the single overriding goal statement for an organization. It focuses all significant organized activities in terms of resources used. The mission statement answers the question, "Why are we doing this at all?" It may be lengthy or brief, but it should describe the enterprise's strategic goal(s) succinctly.

Below are some examples of thoughts that could be included in the mission statement. These are taken from several organizations:

"Our company will be recognized as a world leader in the supply of high quality _____."

"We will produce products that consistently offer the best obtainable value to our customers."

"Our mission is to be the preferred supplier of _____ to European and other international markets."

"Our mission is to always do what is right for our customers. This means providing products of higher value than competitive producers and service comparable to none other."

An outstanding mission statement has been developed by McDonalds Restaurants. It is brief, clear, and "rings with sincerity":

"We will do whatever it takes to deliver a level of quality, service, cleanliness, and value that is so impressive our guests will always choose McDonalds."

The following is a collection of key words commonly used to develop mission statements. They should be used to formulate a legitimate mission statement, not an advertising campaign. The visionary executive and his or her TEAM1 must exercise some prudence in word choice, since the mission statement will truly become the initiative's guiding path.

QUALITY	RELIABILITY	CONSISTENCY
Experience	Superiority	Value
Best	Commitment	Satisfaction
Economical	Service	Involvement
Skill	People	Care
Partners	On-Time	Perfection
Perfect	Continuous	Improvement
Never-Ending	Functional	Constant
Pinnacle	Maximum	Focused
Most	Above Others	Control
Team	Watchful	Cost-Effective
Efficient	Prime	Performance
Ongoing	Teamwork	Obligation
Committed	Constancy	

It takes hours of hard work to reach consensus on the content of a mission statement. However, once it is complete, its effect on the firm and the TQM initiative is significant. Now everyone can see the goal, and understand the company's strategic direction. The mission statement should be signed by the authors, printed on parchment, and placed throughout the business in handsome frames.

Guiding Principles and Values

GUIDING PRINCIPLES AND VALUES describe a set of moral, ethical, and business beliefs that form the base for accomplishing the mission. Although the mission statement may stand alone, most companies (McDonalds is a notable exception) prefer to "flesh it out" with values that give "spirit" to the company's modus operandi. They are daily operating guidelines and long-term indicators of business success. Some principles and values are listed below, categorized by areas of concern.

Customer Concern Values

"We are totally committed to achieving and maintaining quality relationships with customers, suppliers, the community, stockholders, and one another."

"We are dedicated to achieving high quality and total customer satisfaction with continuous improvement."

"We will use a combination of social, technical, and economic principles to achieve new standards of excellence."

"All employees will know their customers, their customers' requirements, and how to meet those requirements."

"We are committed to fulfilling our customers' needs."

"Our success depends on delivering superior products at a competitive price in the market we serve."

"We will actively pursue a renewed understanding of our customer's needs."

"We will actively solicit feedback from our customers."

"We will strive to provide timely follow-up to customer requests."

"Service is paramount in the marketplace and is critical to establishing a reputation for quality."

"We will reward employees who contribute to customer satisfaction."

Business, Management, and Ethical Values

"We will adhere to all ethical and legal guidelines."

"We will apply continuous improvements to achieve world-class status."

"We will work to earn a reasonable profit that encourages growth and assures job security."

"Our products will be manufactured safely, profitably, with a high regard for the community and the environment."

"We will operate with the highest ethical standards at all times."

"Growth and profit are essential for survival."

"Responsibility and authority will be placed at the action level."

"Jobs will be designed to achieve timely feedback."

"Leaders and team members will share accountability in achieving objectives."

"Team objectives will be based on measurable targets."

Employee Contribution and Growth Values

"We consider employees to be our most valuable resource. Their contribution, teamwork, and skill will be the elements from which rewarding work, success, and growth result."

"We will maintain open communication with all employees."

"Every individual's work will be meaningful and important, allowing all workers to reach their fullest potential."

"All employees will be involved in a continuous process that uses systematic problem-solving to achieve improved performance levels. They will also have access to organizational performance data."

"The organization will support all employees and encourage them to enhance their abilities and broaden their contributions to the organization."

"Training is recognized as the key to long-term organizational excellence."

"Training helps people achieve their maximum potential."

"We will offer employees opportunities for professional development."

"We will actively encourage employees to participate in problem-solving processes."

"Training will promote employee flexibility and focus."

"When possible, job descriptions will include management functions, such as planning, controlling, and improving the work process."

"The organization will promote the positive recognition of individual and team performance improvements."

"Everyone in the organization is working toward the same goal."

"We will strive to provide employees at every level with work that is interesting and financially rewarding."

"Wages will be based on acquired skills and job knowledge."

"We are committed to providing all employees with a safe, healthy working environment."

"People are honest and want to work hard."

"People want to know what is expected of them and receive specific evaluation of their performance."

"People want to use their skills and talent."

"People want to be challenged."

Initiative Theme

THE INITIATIVE THEME IS THE NAME of the initiative and a short phrase that succinctly but meaningfully describes the mission statement and principles. It is what will be communicated to vendors, customers, and the outside world.

There are numerous examples of successful themes in today's business and industry, some of which are listed below. As each theme is reviewed, note that the phrase defines the mission and perhaps one or more driving values.

Many popular themes over the past few years have emphasized quality, and use the word liberally:

MOTOROLA–*Quality Means The World To Us;*

XEROX–*Quality You Can Copy;*

FORD–*Quality is Job One;*

HONDA–*Quality For The World, Made In USA;*

LEXUS–*The Relentless Pursuit of Perfection;*

ACURA–*Precision Crafted Performance;* and

PAUL REVERE INSURANCE–*Quality Has Value.*

Another popular approach emphasizes professional performance and skills:

ARTHUR ANDERSEN CONSULTING–*Putting Insight Into Practice;*

OKI PHONES–*You Will Hear The Difference;*

AMERICAN AIRLINES–*Something Special In the Air;*

BELLSOUTH–*Everything You Expect From A Leader;* and

FIDELITY INVESTMENTS–*Common Sense. Uncommon Results.*

The best themes state exactly and clearly the values and principles that guide a company's daily operations. An outstanding example is a quote from Stanley Marcus that describes Nieman-Marcus business values simply and effectively:

"Consumers are statistics. Customers are people."

The initiative theme may also act as a "nickname" for the initiative. An initiative must have a name that is short, explicit, and easily used. Ford's Job1, for example, is a practical and effective nickname that everyone in the organization understands. This is because, in the automotive industry, the term "Job 1" commonly refers to the first car produced on the assembly line after the model year changes. Therefore, the *Quality is Job1* theme suggests quality from the very beginning.

Summary:
The Mission as the Strategic Plan

TODAY MORE EMPHASIS IS being given to formulating an organization's strategic plans, particularly in light of quality and business management problems caused by intense competition with offshore rivals. One failing of US businesses is the inability to see past the current fiscal period when developing strategy. Some cannot even see beyond the current fiscal month.

A properly executed mission statement is an integral part of the company's long-range business plan. It clearly and concisely defines the focus of all business activities for an extended period of time. Although the statement alone does not provide mechanics, it can be used to develop detailed strategic plans. The mission should be the starting point of any business planning session. Any subsequent plans should, in fact, completely complement the mission.

Without a mission, all business plans are simply short-term tactics; the mission forms the basis for true strategy.

CHAPTER 6

SURVEYING THE WORK CLIMATE

*"Men take only their needs into consideration—
never their abilities."*

– NAPOLEON BONAPARTE

FACTS ARE NEEDED TO SUPPORT any scientific study or conclusion. Unfortunately, facts that involve the beliefs, traditions, and attitudes of people are difficult to gather, and people constitute the principal resource in any TQ initiative.

As with any type of manufacturing or business process, an organization's leader must measure progress with some type of criteria. For a finite process or procedure, goals and milestones are quantified and set. Progress is measured by count, weight, volume, time, lines of software code, dollars, pages, or some other scientific parameter. Since the teambuilding process deals with engaging human creativity, progress is much more difficult to assess. Yet it must be done—if the visionary and his or her steering committee are to continue to allocate enterprise resources.

A survey may be used to collect data and information about people in a reasonably organized and scientific manner. There are many types, including:

- personal interviews;
- telephone polls;
- written questionnaires; and
- combinations of instruments.

Surveys may also be taken from seemingly unrelated actions, such as:

- the product counts sold from particular storefront or shelf product displays;
- sales volumes before and after color changes in product packages;
- mail-in coupon offers; and
- other marketing techniques.

Also, manufacturers commonly establish reliable customer databases by using "warranty registration" business-reply postcards for new product sales.

Employees in the workplace are a captive audience; furthermore, most have at least an implied interest in the firm's progress. As a result, forthright and candid written survey questionnaires are usually appropriate for gauging the work climate and evaluating opinions on relevant work issues.

Survey Parameters

QUESTIONS ON ANY TYPE OF SURVEY may deal with at least four human characteristics. These are attitudes, beliefs, behaviors, and attributes.

Attitudes describe how individuals feel about specific ideas, issues, problems, or proposals. Gauging attitudes is highly subjective. Usually survey respondents are offered a scale of responses on which to register emotional "degrees." The typical survey asks how an individual feels, from "strongly agree" to "strongly disagree." "No opinion" or a neutral feeling would be centered on the scale, and moderately strong feelings would be described simply by "agree" or "disagree."

Beliefs show whether an individual thinks something is true or false. This does not necessarily mean "good or bad," but simply whether or not the respondent believes a statement. Generally, a question about a belief is phrased so that "true or false" or "yes or no" are the answers.

Behaviors indicate the actions or directions people will take when confronted with a particular situation. In these questions, people are asked about what course of action they have taken in the past, or will take when certain conditions are met. Behavior questions describe a situation and offer the respondent several logical choices.

Attributes are demographic data or personal information. This data may include the obvious questions about age, job status, sex, years with the employer, race, marital status, and others. If this data is required, respondents must be told that the answers are optional. This protects the legal rights of the respondents. When attribute data is gathered, the survey should be structured to "bracket" response ranges. An example answer to a question about age might be "18 to 25, 26 to 45, 46 to 60," and so forth.

Work Issues

IN THE TYPICAL BUSINESS ENVIRONMENT, most employees have definite opinions in several areas of concern. These form the initial foundation for a survey gauging the work climate and prevailing attitudes. In general, any workplace survey will address these issues in some form:

- *the work itself.* Does the employee perceive work assignments as significant, challenging, rewarding, and worthy of substantial effort?;
- *working conditions.* Does the environment support work performance? Are support services, individuals, departments, and tools and equipment conducive to acceptable performance? Is the work area safe, hygienically acceptable, and environmentally responsible? Is remuneration acceptable and on par with competing businesses?;
- *human resources concerns.* Is the employee treated fairly and equitably? Does the business provide training, skill enhancement, and career progression opportunities? Are there appropriate and fair avenues for redressing formal and informal grievances? Are relations with supervisors satisfactory?; and
- *corporate matters.* How does the employee rate the company? Does the company project a responsible public image? Are policies and procedures definitive and fair? Is the company perceived as a progressive and people-oriented enterprise? Is the company name synonymous with product quality, value, and integrity in customer relations?

Survey Guidelines

POTENTIAL PROBLEMS MAY BE AVOIDED if certain guidelines regarding survey mechanics and logistics are followed. These can also expedite results.

Anonymity. The survey must protect the identity of respondents to assure objective data and maximum feedback. If attribute data is requested on the survey instrument (age, sex, job class, seniority, etc.), it must be stratified or grouped so that individuals cannot be identified based on their answers. All surveys should be distributed at one time, with return requested promptly. Returned surveys should be sealed in unmarked envelopes and deposited at a collection point or placed in the company mail for bulk pickup. Resist the temptation to code the survey or envelope.

Reality. Questions or statements should be based on real, not hypothetical situations. Simple terms, universally understood by the workforce, should be used.

Format. All questions should be close-ended; questions normally should not require an essay response for a response that is not listed. Good questions require answers on a scale, or True/False, Yes/No.

Bias. Select a bias direction. The bias should be either uniformly positive or as neutral as possible. Negative bias sets the stage for additional negativism in response. Most examples in this chapter are neutral or positively-biased from this perspective. Therefore, it is easy to recognize dissatisfaction, or negative responses from the survey.

Follow-up. If an issue emerges as a "sore spot" for most employees, the TQ team should develop a timely response or solution and communicate it to all teams and potential team members. If there are no specific issues or perceived grievances or shortcomings, the TQ steering committee should recap the survey results and communicate them as expediently as possible. All employees must perceive that any workforce survey will be acted upon, positively or negatively.

Surveying Attitudes About TQM

DISCERNING EMPLOYEE PERCEPTIONS before implementing TQ is highly recommended. The visionary executive, his staff, and any outside counselor or consultant should survey existing attitudes about quality and the teambuilding process. Such surveys assess where employees stand on relevant issues, such as team formation and quality matters.

There should be at least two surveys. The first gauges current opinions and perceptions, and shows potential trouble spots or roadblocks. The second, usually identical survey should be done at least a year after the first, to evaluate progress versus the original information.

A TQM employee survey should specifically address the four specific issues of quality, the teambuilding process, relations with others, and relations with the company.

The statements that follow this discussion are presented as typical queries in an employee survey instrument. The statements are grouped by topic: quality, teambuilding, work environment, and company issues. These particular declarations have been used often in employee surveys and are concise and clear. Although the topic areas are grouped together in these examples, the presentation order on a real survey should be randomized. Statements about any one topic are not listed consecutively. As the survey is completed and returned, the data then may be analyzed. Responses to all statements are divided into a five-point scale (fig. 6.1). If the scale is weighted numerically, the greatest disagreement could be 1 and greatest agreement is 5, with 3 being neutral.

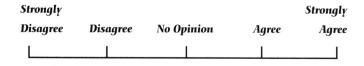

FIGURE 6.1. Response scale for survey questionnaire

Some Statements About Quality

I am concerned about being able to produce a quality product.
My supervisor is concerned with quality problems.
(Company) has high standards for the quality of its products.
I believe the quality of our product could be improved.
I am usually recognized for improvements in quality.

41

The quality level here is as good as in most companies.

The people I work with are concerned with quality.

Quality has improved since I became employed here.

Improved quality will benefit everyone at this company.

Producing a quality product is the most important part of my job.

The quality of our products is generally better than competitors.

I like to be involved with decisions that affect quality.

(Company) produces high-quality products.

There are many possibilities for quality improvement.

Statements About Teambuilding

My co-workers are important to me.

My co-workers usually support me.

I would like more opportunity to work as part of a team.

Our customers appreciate teamwork.

I am proud of being a member of the (Company) team.

Teamwork makes a better product.

I generally like my associates at (Company).

Our team is usually recognized for a job well done.

Teamwork helps organize our business.

The overall (Company) organization is a good working team.

Teamwork decreases the cost of our product.

Our team communicates well.

Teamwork will help me advance in my job.

My department does excellent work.

The people I work with are good team players.

In my work group or department, we are a team.

I believe teamwork helps communication with others.

It is important to have good relations with my work group.

My team members offer assistance when I need it.

Teamwork helps to develop good leaders.

Statements About Work Issues

I enjoy making decisions about work.

I have a reputation for doing excellent work.

I take pride in making improvements to my job.

People at work usually listen to my ideas.

I continuously try to improve my job area.

I enjoy worthwhile accomplishments.

I enjoy the chance to be creative at work.

I constantly try to improve my work.

I am often asked for advice about problems in my department.

I usually schedule my time well.

I usually enjoy my work assignments.

I would like to learn more about what is done in other departments.

Statements About Company Issues

I have opportunities for growth and development at work.

I can usually make changes in the way I perform my job.

I would like to know more about our products and customers.

I am usually recognized for good work.

I receive fair treatment and respect in my job.

We have good planning and organization in my department.

I am usually encouraged to do my best.

I usually receive support and guidance from my supervisor.

I am given sufficient information to perform my job correctly.

I need more training to do my job effectively.

Some of the topics may overlap. Note that there are no references to pay policies, benefit plans, company operating policies or procedures, or any grievance procedures. This set of queries is principally directed at quality and teambuilding issues. Other work environment questions are included only to provide additional data points that verify that responses to the prime issues are reasonable.

Performing a team-related survey before the teambuilding and training process is of utmost importance since survey results will uncover shortcomings that may be specifically addressed by training. For example, a survey might show that employees wrongly believe their company's products are "second-rate" or only marginal in quality. If that is so, it may be worthwhile to disseminate information about market share, customer plaudits, and competitor's product quality. If internal relations are perceived as stressful, additional communications efforts may be in order. The survey must be done to provide valuable data that will help the TQ effort.

Summary

ATTITUDE SURVEYS ARE NECESSARY for assessing the progress of the TQ initiative and teambuilding. They need not be lengthy or complex; they should simply ask for honest opinions. Few operating managers and teambuilding consultants have the psychological expertise to design surveys. It is therefore probably sufficient to select thirty to fifty simple and meaningful questions. Be honest and communicate results clearly. Repeat the same survey a year or more after teams have been operating.

If teambuilding and TQ activities have been successful, it will be obvious in the survey results. Following the first experiences, fine-tune the survey, keep good records, and continue surveys annually or biannually to keep abreast of team issues.

CHAPTER 7

ALL ABOUT TEAMS

"If we let our people flourish and grow, if we use the best ideas they come up with, then we have the chance to win. The idea of liberation and empowerment of our work force is not enlightenment—it's a competitive necessity. When you look at the global arena, that's what our competitive advantage is."

– JACK WELCH

TEAMS ARE THE CENTER of any TQM initiative. They can effectively harness workforce knowledge in any enterprise. As sports teams depend on the participation of all members, so also do TQ teams. With participation and some initial modest successes, a synergy for more challenge is created. As in sports, the sum of individual talents is surpassed by accomplishments and pride in the whole unit.

One useful definition of a team is: "A number of people who have been organized to work together to produce high quality results that will benefit each individual and to the parent organization."

In other words, a team is a group of individuals that relate directly to get things done. Essential to accomplishing with one another the group's work objectives, however, is the intrinsic good humor, fun, and working relationships created by teamwork and team bonding dynamics.

Groups vs. Teams

IN AMERICAN INDUSTRY, A RECENT trend has been to recognize and promote participative employee groups. This has perhaps been brought about in part by reluctance to supervise, measure, and reward (or reprimand) performance at the individual level. In many organizations, managers are satisfied with group performance, and do not explore beyond aggregate group measures of productivity and quality. In those enterprises that have instituted a team concept, however, the results are far superior with the same or even fewer resources. A team climate generally improves every aspect of performance.

There are significant differences between groups of employees and teams. Employees are typically groups of individuals placed in a function or department for the utility and convenience. They may have nothing more in common than an interest in a reasonable wage and job security. The following discussion offers a brief but noteworthy comparison of groups and teams. Recognize, however, that all positive traits of the team environment are difficult to achieve consistently, and that they reflect ideal conditions.

The following behaviors are typically seen in work groups:
- individuals in the group occasionally work at odds with others in the group; they may not have similar understandings of goals;
- members have a poor view of the goals and results expected within the group. Each individual tends to focus on his or her own desires and expectations and works toward objectives not always clearly identified. There is little sense of urgency;
- group members are externally directed and have little input in daily group problem-solving activities. There may be many individuals working in different directions on the same task. Group members are focused on tasks rather than common goals;
- communications are poor. Since commonality of purpose is rare, mistrust and suspicion of others in and outside the group are harbored;
- there is little continuity. Group members focus exclusively on their best outcomes for each day. Group members may be described as "independent" or "overdependent." They do not depend on their peers;

• groups are run autocratically. Conflicts may be ignored or handled incorrectly, either by the supervisor or group members. On-going emotional damage may occur as opinions are kept hidden;

• training is not utilized fully, due to peer opinions or pressures. Supervisors are not given prompt feedback and frequently discover group problems through the "grapevine";

• there is little creativity and innovation. Since the group does not see the advantages of new ideas, members are content to "roll with the punches";

• group discussion and consensus on issues are rare. Decisions are frequently made hastily by senior or more vocal members of the group; and

• groups tolerate others in the workplace and their work tasks. Group members avoid risk and adopt complacency.

In contrast, team behaviors exhibit much more positive influences. These are a few:

• members recognize their interdependence and understand that personal and team goals are best accomplished with mutual support. Turf struggles dissipate; personal gains at the expense of others become less important. As in sports, individual goals are subservient to "winning the game";

• members have ownership of their positions and individual performance goals and expectations because they help establish them. Team members focus on clear team goals; teams are innovative; this is a result of their being given an opportunity to use their skills and unique talents for the good of the organization;

• teams practice participative management. Members work in a climate of mutual trust and respect. They encourage themselves, and are encouraged by supervisors, to express and discuss ideas, feelings, opinions, and problems openly; communication between team members and others in the organization is open, frequent, and honest. Clarifications are made when requested;

• developing skills and training are encouraged. The team supports each member's accomplishments. The team readily uses newly acquired problem-solving tools;

- teams act to resolve conflicts quickly. All members recognize that disagreements take time that could otherwise be spent productively. The team members know when to request outside help to resolve a situation;
- decisions are made by consensus, after all opinions and facts have been heard; and
- teams are self-starters, rather than "kick starters." They realize that the team's success is vital to the organization's success, and vice-versa. Teams enjoy their work and their peers. Teams like a challenge.

There is a clear test for determining the degree of teamwork in any organization; it connects organizational success with team success. In short, what happens when a work group successfully completes an important project? If nothing happens, then it is not a team. It is simply another group that cannot be distinguished from any other loose collection of people.

Team Member Roles

TEAM MEMBERS HAVE INTIMATE contact or knowledge of the project, product, or area under consideration or study. As employees, and as TQ partners, they have responsibilities and duties to the organization, the team leader, their work group, and themselves. They must adhere to the following credo:

- team members must acknowledge that company management has indicated concern by establishing the TQ initiative and building teams. Team members should consider their participation a priority, not an intrusion on workplace positions. The team is now a part of the "real job";
- individuals must contribute all knowledge and abilities to the success of the initiative. They must share their experience and expertise. They must participate in all meetings and discussions, even on topics outside their immediate areas. They should not be shy about asking questions; each person must clearly understand every detail of the business or manufacturing process that is under review; and
- members must carry out assignments between meetings. This

may include observing processes, gathering data, interviewing others, charting data, writing reports, and so forth.

Team members should be coached and counseled in techniques that will contribute to their development. Emphasis should be placed on:

- setting team goals and working as a team toward those goals;
- being receptive and open-minded toward new ideas;
- listening and being receptive of the views of others;
- providing constructive input to the team; and
- supporting the team leader, other members, and facilitator in their efforts to present ideas to management.

Benefits of Teams

A TEAM IS A FLEXIBLE AND COMPETENT business tool that can support a positive management strategy in numerous ways:

- management of complexity. The knowledge and resources available to a team enables it to manage complex situations creatively. Trained teams use their membersí diverse skills and backgrounds to respond to difficult problems;
- rapid response. If a technical or specific problem is within the group's province, well-developed mature teams are capable of responding rapidly and effectively. Of course, the team must have time available for the meetings and actions needed to address the problem;
- high motivation. The team feeds on the needs for acceptance, belonging, and recognition. Mature team members will eventually downplay formal organizational recognition in favor of peer acceptance and kudos for tasks well done; good quality decisions. Mature teams generally can make informed decisions of better quality than individuals can. Also, the level of commitment to team decisions is higher; and
- collective strength. This might also be defined as "synergy." The individual strengths of the team create a greater effect when applied through the team. Dealing with other departments and functional groups usually is more productive when a strong

49

group's collective strengths and "negotiating power" support a consensus action.

Teambuilding Issues

TEAMBUILDING IS THE PROCESS OF DELIBERATELY creating and structuring a team. It takes time, planning, and deliberate progression. Each team must eventually answer these six questions:

1. What's in it for us (me)?
2. What is the object of this organization?
3. Who's in charge?
4. Who cares about our work anyway?
5. What resources do we have to do our work?
6. Where are we in the organization?

A significant question asked immediately by every team member is the first: each individual must believe there is definite career advantage or tangible reward in team activity. The other questions must be answered to the members' satisfaction as the group's activities progress.

The process for achieving satisfaction with the team's organization may take numerous meetings and project completions. With the help of a facilitator and a trained leader, team members will have deliberately worked through each issue or roadblock and transitioned from a work group to an effective team.

Motives for Teambuilding

SEVERAL MOTIVES OR DESIRES MAY FORM the base for a business to adopt a team-oriented working structure. Some positive and success-oriented motives include:

- a pragmatic and visionary management that wishes to use a system to solve problems and run the enterprise;
- new management personnel who wish to be accepted rapidly into an established business structure;
- a perceived need to marshal the collective creativity and

commitment of the workforce to meet new challenges and demands. These might well be dissipating market share or new competitors;
  • a need to resolve problems of relationships, commitment, or lack of clarity in work goals communicated throughout the organization; and
  • a perceived need to generate new life and enthusiasm in the organization.
Some negative motives might include the following:
  • initiation from a head corporate office or other external source without the local workforce's support and commitment;
  • increasing management's level of manipulation and control of the workforce. This may include using team programs as a ruse or ploy in union–management relations; and
  • instituting an initiative because it is seen as the current and correct "thing to do."
These views will not support an effective, successful, long-term initiative.

The Team Development Process

ANY ACTIVITY THAT IMPROVES OPERATING EFFECTIVENESS and issue resolution may be considered team development. It may be evaluated by examining how the team functions in each of five general areas, and taking appropriate remedial action if problems are noted. The areas of interest are:
  • the work environment. This is the effect influences outside the team have on its operation and effectiveness. This includes procedures, systems, organization structures, customer initiatives, and so forth;
  • the team mission. In short, this is what the team does. How are goals set? Are goals and objectives clear? Is there commitment among the team members and in the overall organization? Is there consensus and agreement on the results expected from team interaction?;
  • roles and assignments. In short, who does what? Are roles clearly defined? Do team members know the contributions

51

expected of themselves and others? Are there conflicts arising from overlapping responsibility or authority?;

• operating procedures. Policies and procedures define the team's boundaries. They contribute substantially to the group's effectiveness in conducting meetings, planning, and recording actions, and using problem–solving tools. For this reason, some degree of formally imposed procedures from the steering committee are suggested; and

• work relationships. This is the effect interpersonal relationships formed by company management, supervisory staff, team leaders, facilitators, and team members have on team effectiveness.

Team development must be assessed periodically by the team leader, facilitator, and business managers. Such reviews determine progress and additional needs like coaching, training, or reorganization. If the team has not matured to the point where it needs little or no facilitation, it may regress.

Stages of Team Development

THERE ARE FOUR PHASES OF TEAM GROWTH and maturation. These are: testing, infighting, organizing, and maturity. Some authors have referred to these four stages as "forming, storming, norming, and performing." Other terms include "orientation, operation, realization, and production." All forms of terminology recognize at least four distinct phases of "comfort" and effectiveness in the group. The phases are not well defined and vary in length and intensity with each group observed.

TESTING *(forming, orientation)*

In this phase, people try to find their positions in the group. There may be apprehension, fear, discomfort, and a general reticence. As time progresses, there is personal exchange and contact, until each participant decides his or her position and "comfort level."

INFIGHTING *(storming, operation)*

As the team develops, sorting out power and influence relationships becomes necessary. Alliances are formed and certain individuals gain leadership or other significant roles. The team's formal leader must exercise authority and cohesive direction or the team will falter.

The team also has to decide how it will operate. In essence, all issues are concerned with control, and three questions must be answered:

- Who controls the team (internally and externally)?
- How is control exercised (e.g., autocracy, consensus, accommodation, compromise)?
- What are the penalties for non-compliance with team standards (what happens to "delinquents")?

ORGANIZING *(norming, realization)*

When control issues are at least temporarily resolved, the team begins to tackle its work with renewed energy. By this time, team members have generally committed themselves to making the team successful. This is an important time for support from the organization at large, so that all members know their efforts are being observed and appreciated. Outside recognition is particularly important.

Generally, the team does its work smoothly in this phase; members listen to and show respect for one another. The group's capability for handling problems creatively and effectively strengthens. This is the time to provide the team with any training and procedural information it needs to be successful.

MATURITY *(performing, production)*

Closeness and rapport characterize a fully established team. Members are prepared to extend themselves for their associates. Typically, they enjoy their meetings and their interactions with one another. Each member becomes protective of group integrity. The team contributes to the effectiveness of the entire organization and to quality, productivity, safety, schedules, cost and other measurable parameters.

It is tempting to offer less outside support to the mature team; however, this should not be the case. Support keeps the team objectives focused and keeps the team role in the organization clear.

An Effective Team

A MATURE AND EFFECTIVE TEAM has been painstakingly built. Problems have been worked out, relationships deepened, and roles clarified. Successful and effective teams normally exhibit the following characteristics:

- appropriate leadership. The team leader has adequate skills and devotes the time necessary to build the team. He or she also shares or relinquishes leadership to others as they become qualified to assume the management task;
- suitable membership. The team members are individually qualified. They are capable of providing the mix of expertise and knowledge needed to make the team work;
- commitment to the team. Team members are individually committed to the team's goals and principles. They willingly devote personal energy to building the team and supporting other team members. Team members proudly represent the group in external settings;
- constructive climate. The team has developed a working climate. Members feel relaxed, can be direct and open, and are prepared to take risks;
- concern for achievement. The team's objectives are clear and members feel they are worthwhile. Team energies are devoted to achieving results. Goals are challenging but achievable;
- clear organizational role. The team knows the corporate and local business unit goals. It has a distinct and productive role in the overall organizationís plan to achieve those goals;
- effective work methods. The team has developed systematic and effective methods for planning, attacking, and solving problems;
- well-organized team procedures. Communications and administrative procedures are well defined and documented. Accomplishments are readily communicated;
- positive intergroup relations. Positive relationships exist between the team and other working areas, departments, and teams. Individuals work with and keep in contact with other teams for the common good;
- critique without recrimination. Weaknesses and errors are examined and corrected without personal accusation or attack. The team collectively learns from experience;
- creative strength. New ideas from individuals or groups inside or outside the immediate organization are also

supported. Taking innovative risks is rewarded. The team can develop new ideas by interacting; and

• acceptance of external direction. The team readily accepts critique, instruction, or direction and recognizes contributions from external facilitators or managers.

Effective vs. Ineffective teams

MANY FACTORS INFLUENCE THE GROWTH and effectiveness of teams. These may be so intertwined that analysis and a single, definitive "yes or no" answer about team productivity become difficult. The following list summarizes characteristics that define well-functioning teams and those that may experience difficulty. The team leader and facilitator must reduce or elimi-nate potential problem areas as much as he or she can. The characteristics are grouped by those areas that influence team development:

Work environment. Teams need regularly scheduled meetings at the same location. Effective teams are equipped with the skills and resources necessary to complete tasks. Ineffective teams do not have, or have not been given, adequate resources. They are often the victims of poor sched-uling, and ill-equipped or unavailable meeting rooms.

Team mission. Effective teams know their parent organizationís mission, and have one of their own. Their mission definition is based on team goals and objectives the team has agreed on and the schedule and priorities nec-essary for accomplishing the goals. Ineffective teams have not reached a development consensus, their objectives are unclear, and they have not determined schedules. Everyone "does their own thing," and communica-tion with the main group and the overall organization is poor.

Team member roles. In an effective team, roles are clearly defined and do not overlap. Team leadership is strong; the leader communicates with each member. Team leaders and members are available for assistance when there are misunderstandings. On an ineffective team, responsibilities are poorly defined and may overlap. There is no clear leader, no direction for a given task, and "passing the buck" is prevalent. There may be "power plays." Members may act independently, ignoring the interdependence needed for the team to function.

Procedural matters. Effective teams are operated by consensus in meetings that are task-and improvement-oriented. Meeting emphasis is on problem-solving, not finding scapegoats or placing blame. Normally, all team members take part in the discussion. They prepare for each meeting, take notes, listen well, and give each other feedback. Ineffective teams make decisions in a crisis mode. Communications are generally "one way," from the top down and are dominated by one or a few. Meetings are generally unproductive, with endless debates over minor or unimportant points. Team members may be late, uninformed and delinquent with assigned action items;

Personal relationships. Effective teams have identity and pride. Conflicts are not personal and are viewed as part of the decision-making process. Difficult issues are discussed openly, without personal attacks or vendettas. On effective teams, members enjoy working through complex problems with each other. There is mutual respect. Ineffective team members do not want to be identified with the team. There are both open and covert conflicts among members, and, in the extreme case, serious altercations. By nature, the members of ineffective teams compete with others on the team, not against a common goal or problem.

Team Goals

A TEAM EXISTS WHEN MEMBERS are working toward a common goal they have identified themselves. It is also important that teams identify those tasks that do not need team action since some members may have individual objectives outside the team's scope. An effective team is aware of the following:

Goals are necessary for the team to function. They also must be clear, concise, understood, and agreed-to by all team members. When each member is asked to identify the goals of the team, the responses should be consistent. If team members interpret the goals differently, their directions may diverge. That could cause conflict and a lower level of teamwork.

Team members must share goal ownership. Members must participate in setting team goals and they must be committed to them. If goals are mandated from the top, team members should then be allowed to decide how they will be accomplished. The degree of goal ownership and the amount of energy expended on reaching goals are mainly determined by how much the team participated in their creation.

Goals must be measurable and attainable. Goals should be well defined and quantified if possible. They should be specific enough to allow members to recognize when they have accomplished them. They should be demanding and credible, offering the team a chance to work through challenges in unison.

Goals must be shared by the team. On many teams, members do not share their goals with one another. They are not clearly understood by all members. Members must know what others are trying to accomplish, the possible impact upon them, and how their actions can help or hinder.

Conflicts must be resolved. Occasionally, the goals of team members will conflict. In these cases the team leader and facilitator must act promptly to point the team in a common direction. The team energies they waste can be avoided with an "up-front" discussion, understanding, and consensus.

The team members' attitudes toward TQ and its goals are critical if the continuous improvement initiative is to succeed. The best leadership, goals, and procedures are meaningless without commitment from each contributor.

CHAPTER 8

ORGANIZING EMPLOYEE TEAMS FOR TQM

*"A group becomes a team when each member
is sure enough of himself and his contribution
to praise the skills of the others."*

– NORMAN G. SHIDLE

OF ALL THE FACTORS ESSENTIAL to the success of the initiative, instilling cooperation and motivation in the workforce is one of the most critical. All employees, from rank-and-file through senior management, must "buy into" the TQM process at its inception and support it as it evolves.

Since they have seen various programs come and go during their employment, many employees will likely ask, "what's in it for me?" It is a good question, and one not easily answered. As TQM teams are formed, the managers, supervisors, facilitators, and consultants must continually strive to emphasize how the initiative will benefit them. Individual employees and their work groups have legitimate questions that must be answered completely and truthfully.

Even if the question is answered satisfactorily for most employees, there will still be hard-core cynics and skeptics denigrating the initiative. Every executive, team leader, manager, supervisor, facilitator, and consultant involved should immediately put these critics into separate personal mental "buckets" and vow not to let them derail the initiative. After some time has progressed and as teams congeal into effective problem-solving units, most skeptics will decide to participate. If they do not, the team process must continue without them.

What's In It For Me?

AT THE EMPLOYEE LEVEL, "what's in it for me?" is the driving question. At the very least, a successful TQM implementation can bring individuals these benefits:

- long-term job security is enhanced because the company and employee improve relations with existing customers and open new avenues for additional business;
- the teambuilding process provides new learning opportunities. At the very least, the TQM process will expose employee teams to problem-solving techniques, techniques for building group and personal interactions, and opportunities for "making a difference";
- TQM provides an opportunity for renewed employee communication with peers, with the work group, the department, and several tiers of management;
- success fosters reward. The active TQ team player will have opportunities for career advancement. Individuals and teams are also rewarded with cash and merchandise incentives if their quality and productivity improvements are successful (see Chap. 13);
- TQM success drives employee empowerment. As TQ successes accumulate, the work environment becomes increasingly receptive to greater responsibility and authority at all job levels. The success of continuous improvement initiatives also provides employees with more involvement in operations; and
- TQM promotes pride and satisfaction in the workplace. Successful TQ initiatives instill a new level of enthusiasm and employee self-satisfaction. Lost humor is found again, and the majority of employees look forward to the renewed challenges of their employment. For many, working is "fun" again.

Team Size

AS TEAM MEMBERS ARE DESIGNATED and teams start to organize for the tasks ahead, some consideration must be given to the questions of team size and structure. These two factors will have considerable effect on the progress and success of the team.

Much revolves around the leader's ability to control, the nature of the personalities in the group, and the nature of the problems under discussion. As a rule of thumb, an initial team activity would not be hindered by a group size of under ten. As the size decreases from seven or six, however, there is some visible loss in the level of discussion and "synergy." Further, another danger in a smaller group is that it can create an "elite" class that might pose problems for new members in the future.

The best team size is any size the team leader is capable of handling, up to a reasonable extreme. Teams with as many as fifteen participants have been successful, but this is not the norm. Some authors and individuals that have served as team leaders and facilitators have ten or less, and one source says "seven plus or minus two" is the answer.

Except during special projects and ad hoc tasks, team size should be limited to ten, with seven or eight the optimum.

Team Organization

EVERY TEAM HAS ESSENTIAL CHARACTERISTICS, regardless of business or industry and the product or service offered. Firstly, the team must have a designated leader. Leadership must be an established, formal position, with many defined responsibilities. Although the leadership of a group may change over time, there is no such thing as "informal" or "rotating" leadership.

Second, there must be a facilitator. This is an objective and responsible "third party" concerned with teamwork and problem-solving procedures. A facilitator has many responsibilities (see Chapter 10 for a more definitive discussion), but the prime directive is that he or she establish an atmosphere for a successful team process. The facilitator is concerned only with process, not content.

Finally, there are the team members themselves. Apart from considering team composition (see the discussion of natural work groups), team members must be given an opportunity to create, innovate, learn, inspire, and advance as a consequence of their team experience. Every opportunity for advancement must be offered, including appointment as the team leader of their "home" team, leadership of another team, or facilitator to another group.

One viable form of team organization is shown in figure 9.1. It could be called a "tiered" or "overlapped" system of team organization. It is especially workable because it affords each team visibility and communication through all administrative layers. A hierarchy of three teams is shown for illustration purposes, but the structure is applicable to any number of layers. Further, an internal or external initiative consultant or facilitator is available to all hierarchy levels at any time, and typically attends most team meetings in the early stages.

Role of Participant

Participant	Tier 1 Team	Tier 2 Team	Tier 3 Team
Employee	Member	----	----
First-line Supervisor	**Leader**	**Member**	----
Manager	Facilitator	Leader	Member
Senior Manager	----	Facilitator	**Leader**
Executive	----	----	Facilitator

FIGURE 9.1. *Tiered Team Organization*

As shown, the leader for each team is a team member of the next highest team tier. Each team leader becomes the facilitator of the next lowest team in the tier. Thus, individuals must look at content when functioning as leaders or team members and process when functioning as facilitators. This type of organization also encourages communication among groups, and between management and the workforce. Each team's leader is assisted by the team facilitator, who will be the next level supervisor or manager.

Additional tiers that include more administrative levels, up to and including the president, CEO, or chairman of a company, are conceivable. A corporation chairman of the board of directors could facilitate the executive staff meetings being led by the CEO or President. At every tier, an outside consultant or specialist is available as an ex officio facilitator. Eventually, teams will not need outside intervention, but it should be available during the formative process.

Overall, this type of team structure has many significant advantages. These include better communication and the potential for cross-training individuals as facilitators and leaders. Further, it allows management almost complete access to the workings and progress of individual teams and prompts more active involvement.

The Natural Work Group

WHEN TEAM SIZE AND COMPOSITION are being considered, an important factor is "natural" work assignments. In a natural work group or team, individuals that have worked together regularly are given the opportunity to continue relationships in a problem-solving TQM team. For example, members of an operating team for a sophisticated machine might logically become the TQ team for that area. Maintenance people on a given shift or crew might become a TQ team, or those operators associated with a JIT- or flexible manufacturing cell might be teammates.

Creating TQM teams from natural work groups has advantages that seem to outweigh the negatives. The natural work group approach also has advantages over alternative "cross-functional" or "inter-disciplinary" teams. A few of these advantages are dicussed below.

Communication links are established in natural work groups. The members of the group usually have no problems expressing their feelings to one another. With some refinement, there can be an excellent interplay of ideas and creativity. Teams whose members have no prior personal associations must build in extra time for developing rapport and camaraderie.

An innate "pecking order" has been established. Any social group has superior and subordinate members. In an already formed group there is no need to spend time sorting out the membership hierarchy. Instead, more time can be committed to building the team role in TQ. As training and teambuilding commence, subordinate group members will find new occasions to challenge superior tiers. Eventually, roles within the group may change completely.

A natural group has a natural leader. Initially, this is the immediate supervisor; however, that may change as the group matures. Using a supervisor as a team leader will undoubtedly be a challenge to the team and the leader, but there is no one more qualified to plan, direct, organize, and monitor group progress. Of course, the supervisor must also be able to assume the role of a participative team player.

Natural work groups know most about their immediate area. A team's collective creativity and synergy are a superior force when it must address a technical problem in its work area. Cross-functional or inter-disciplinary teams, despite their other strengths, cannot act with the same speed.

Team Assignment

CONTRARY TO SOME OPINIONS, PARTICIPATION in TQM teams cannot be a volunteer activity. This was one failing of early "quality circles" programs; in some installations, prospective participants were given the opportunity to volunteer for team service. Occasionally, some refused, much to the chagrin of management and other, more enlightened employees. Non-participation is an instant roadblock, put in place before the initiative gets off the ground. Initially, all employees must participate on the teams established in their respective areas.

In most installations, employees are paid for the time spent in employee team meetings, and for all other team-based activities. This is the way the initiative should operate. Employees need not be coerced to participate, but they must be present at team meetings and activities. Eventually, even the most hardened skeptic will see the initiative's value, but in the interim the team leader, team facilitator, and members cannot allow the naysayer(s) to derail team activities.

Problem employees should not receive extra attention in the team setting; this plainly focuses on the individual, perhaps satisfying his or her perverse need for attention. If coaching or counseling is suggested, the team leader, with appropriate assistance from the facilitator or outside consultant, should perform it away from the team setting. The employee should be allowed to continue attending meetings unless he or she interrupts them and proves to be a sociopathic problem. At this juncture, the employee may be allowed some latitude. In any case, the offender should always be kept informed of meeting notices, minutes, and other collective team actions, particularly successes and kudos. In no case should any team member be reprimanded for non-participation. This is a clear de-motivator.

Team Meeting Logistics

THE SUCCESS OF THE TQ AND CONTINUOUS improvement initiatives is based on the team members fulfilling their individual and group missions. This occurs at the grass-roots level, which is typically a weekly meeting in which work priorities, goals, actions, and problems are discussed and actions are assigned.

Each meeting must meet a few criteria:
- the meeting day, time, and location should be fixed if possible;
- the acknowledged team leader must be present. If for some reason, this is not possible, he or she must have appointed a substitute and provided that person with an agenda;
- a facilitator must be present;
- a quorum (or simple majority) of the group must be present;
- the meeting must be run in an orderly manner. Full parliamentary procedures are probably unnecessary, but order is essential for conducting business in a limited time;
- an action register of some type must be maintained that assigns names to projects and individuals to follow-up actions;
- the group secretary must keep notes of meeting progress; each meeting should address the status and progress of every open action item, and no items should be skipped or ignored;
- meeting length should generally be limited to one hour. In early organizational efforts, longer sessions are not unusual, but these are an exception; and
- the meeting facility must be conducive to productivity. A clean, comfortable conference room should be selected and made available for regular team meetings. Noisy, poorly ventilated or marginally lighted areas should be avoided.

65

Meeting Rules

REGULAR IN-PLANT MEETINGS are the principal tool for fulfilling the team role and developing problem-solving techniques. Generally, the time is quite limited, and productivity demands that meetings be conducted with efficiency.

A code of meeting conduct can often prevent difficulties by establishing rules for "law and order" in the team infrastructure. The following code of conduct was adopted by a typical manufacturing team:

Be on time.

Be prepared.

Bring paper, pencil, and other needed items.

Be responsible for your assignments.

Pay attention and participate.

The majority rules.

Listen; do not interrupt or criticize.

Be courteous, cooperative, and fair, and respect each other's
    feelings and confidentiality.

Help with setup and cleanup.

No smoking.

Have FUN.

Listening Skills

FOR TEAMS TO FUNCTION AT THEIR FULLEST potential, it is essential that all members listen effectively. An effective approach to improving listening skills involves a few simple guidelines.

Concentration is important. Team members must pay full attention to the topic and listen intently to the speakers at hand. Outside noises, job concerns, or daydreaming are distractions that can affect concentration. The team leader should reduce or eliminate physical distraction and competing noises if possible. In some environments, this may include turning off portable radios or telephones and posting a "do not disturb" sign on the meeting room door.

Avoid premature evaluations. Team members should be encouraged to restrain their natural bias toward a particular topic so that a fair assessment may be made by the entire team after all the facts are in. Hasty, negative judgments can hurt or prevent further discussion and focused listening.

Avoid faking attention. Some individuals pretend they are hearing and analyzing every word or point in a discussion or presentation. Fortunately, there are few who can feign effective listening for extended periods. Body language usually signals or lack of interest. The leader or facilitator should watch for signs of disinterest, such as coughing, shifting leg or body positions, "doodling" on scrap paper, and so forth.

Hold back emotions. Sometimes listeners will experience intense emotions (positive and negative) in response to certain language or topics. Team members should try to moderate their emotion. This reduces conflict and misunderstanding. Those introducing sensitive topics should moderate their language, as well.

Don't get wrapped up in detail. When a complex or technical subject is being presented, look for the major ideas and points. Try not to take copious notes. If there is a problem in how an idea is interpreted, discuss it as a side issue or with other team members.

Don't take anything personally. Listening becomes difficult when a team member takes offense at a comment and responds defensively. Some individuals respond without realizing it; others miss important points while they mentally plan a response to a perceived personal attack. These techniques indicate that team members have not yet learned to look beyond individual interests. Objectivity and logic should be stressed.

Cautions

THE VISIONARY EXECUTIVE AND THE TQ steering committee must provide the new teams with opportunity, resource, knowledge, and guidance so that a self-sustaining and self-nurturing entity that will survive and prosper is created. In the teambuilding process, it is important to allow enough time for teams and individuals to absorb their new roles and learning so they may avoid potential pitfalls. A few cautions are in order.

Provide orientation. Give new teams concise and specific directions on the current climate, expectations, and directions. Management must also provide clear behavior models.

Provide adequate resources. This means time and money. Recognize early and completely that substantial investment is necessary before there can be meaningful payback or reward. Culture changing is not cheap.

Establish management credibility. Credibility is an important asset. Team members must have faith in management's knowledge, believability, and business approach. Until a manager's view is respected, his credibility is clouded. Teambuilding and TQ cannot use a *"do as I say, not as I do"* philosophy.

Don't force issues. Readiness for TQM and team approaches must be assessed early in the initiative. There may be a number of unresolved employee issues that, unless allowed to "ventilate," will create roadblocks. Many employees will suspect that managers and supervisors have "hidden agendas" if proper planning steps are not taken early on.

Provide professional assistance where needed. Few organizations have complete internal capabilities for organizing and training personnel in team principles and TQ techniques. Organize a thorough selection process and contract with a qualified consultant or facilitation specialist, even if only for a review and assessment of the plans for the initiative.

End involvement when appropriate. Slowing and then ending the involvement of organizational outsiders with team activities demonstrates trust in the team. When teams are functioning independently and with enthusiasm and results, back off. Occasional audits are certainly acceptable, but you should make it clear to teams that they have authority and responsibility to function at given levels without restraint.

Clarify intergroup relationships. No single team will exist in a vacuum; communication with other teams, departments, and business functions is critical. Teams and leaders must know where their group fits in the overall TQ plan and at what levels they must relate or report. There will certainly be "effective" and "ineffective" teams, but no team should have the luxury of predominance or independence. There is no place for elitism or separatism.

Enforce accountability. Make budgets and other commitments clear; the team has finite limits for available resources and must, as any manager, stay within planned expenditures. The "buck stops" with the team leader.

CHAPTER 9

TEAM LEADERSHIP
AND FACILITATION

*"Good leaders are visionaries with a poorly developed
sense of fear and no concept of the odds against them.
They make the impossible happen."*

– DR. ROBERT JARVIK

BECAUSE TEAM LEADERS AND FACILITATORS share certain responsibilities in a TQ and teambuilding initiative, it may be tempting to choose one person to fulfill both roles. This is a mistake. Two individuals are needed. This chapter discusses why.

Natural Leaders

CHOOSING SOMEONE TO FILL A TEAM leadership position is an important decision. The visionary executive and the TQ steering committee should carefully screen individuals. In a TQ initiative, leaders are truly "made," not "born," but the candidates must have certain innate leadership characteristics.

Ideally, the initial team leaders are the natural leaders in their work groups (see Chap. 8). Usually, these individuals are first-line supervisors or salaried section or group leaders who have already demonstrated a propensity for planning, organizing, and leading groups. These natural leaders should be given the additional training and insight they need to become TQ leaders.

First and foremost, a supervisor must see his or her role as a coach or facilitator to a group of people and not as a director or taskmaster. In a non-TQ environment, most supervisors are concerned with the essentials of production (cost, schedule, and quality) as well as daily planning and "firefighting" activities. As the leader of both a natural work group and a functioning TQ team, the former supervisor must develop new social skills that match his or her technical and supervisory expertise.

For many supervisors, meeting weekly, setting common goals, and agreeing on work-related issues is a tall order. If the supervisor cannot commit to becoming the leader of a team, rather than the leader of a department, then it may be necessary to select another individual.

Team Leadership Qualities

IF A CANDIDATE IS TO BECOME a successful team leader, he or she must be both willing and able to:
- work as a team, rather than as an individual;
- make the commitment necessary to ensure team success;
- represent the team in events and presentations with other groups, including local and corporate management;
- provide training, counsel, and guidance to others;
- work with an internal or external consultant or facilitator to assure team progress;
- distance themselves from personal or other unrelated issues; and
- set and work toward goals.

Leadership in Operation

EFFECTIVE DAY-TO-DAY LEADERSHIP IS essential if a team is to function successfully. Effective leaders strengthen both the teambuilding process and the completing of team tasks. They also have a continuing positive effect on the climate, which can lead to even greater accomplishments. Team leaders have an immense social and technical obligation imposed on them.

Effective team leaders must practice the following fundamentals daily. They must:

- care about people and respect them as individuals. Leaders must believe that people are essentially motivated to do a good job. They must deal fairly and consistently with everyone and act as they expect others to act. They must be open, forthright, and consistently do what they say they are going to do. When they can't, they must explain why not;
- strive for continuous improvements in themselves and in their relationships with others;
- treat the leadership assignment as a fundamental part of his or her daily responsibilities;
- be dedicated to improving people's work lives, their safety, and their productivity;
- be willing to coach and advise without being despotic;
- believe that when their teams do well, they will share credit. Conversely, he or she must also demonstrate their support for the teams and individuals when things are not going smoothly;
- support team efforts and help the team when it is needed. Effective leaders seek out education, training, and development activities for team members, including themselves;
- keep themselves and members of the teams aware of other teams' needs, as well as those of internal and external customers. This includes meeting regularly with peers on other teams to exchange information and ideas openly. It also means seeking outside information that pertains to his or her team and sharing it regularly;
- solicit ideas and listen carefully when they are offered; and
- conduct themselves with pride as professional representatives of their respective organizations.

Dimensions of Leadership

TEAM LEADERSHIP MUST BE CONSTRAINED and guided by ground rules. If a team leader (i.e., supervisor) is to be held accountable for his or her team's

71

work, he or she must have a number of rights. The leader must have the resources available to protect both team and individual interests when the group is functioning.

There are no such things as "co-leaders." At any given time, there should be only one person serving as a team's official leader. It may seem more egalitarian to share leadership rights, but in reality, this concept has created many traps.

The TQ steering committee must choose the team's first leader. A team must be cohesive with several successes behind it before it can make such a deliberate decision.

The leader must have the absolute right to veto even is he or she is not an organizational supervisor. It is best to avoid this situation, but some-times it is necessary.

The leader must have the latitude to delegate action items. He or she must also be able to assign reasonable deadlines and hold individuals or sub-groups responsible for their agreed-to actions. If the team's output is unsatisfactory, the leader must decide what actions to take.

The leader has the right to remove any team member incapable of fruitful work with other teammates. This should be a last resort–taken only after every conflict resolution technique has been employed and outside inter-vention has failed. The offender is not "fired," but will simply continue their daily work duties in the same department and area. If the offender is from another department, the leader must be able to contact the cognizant super-visor or manager for assistance. Communications with outside departments on issues involving individuals should be coordinated with the steering com-mittee and an outside facilitator.

The Team Facilitation Process

TQM TEAMS GENERALLY FUNCTION more effectively when individuals experi-enced in management, human resources, and problem-solving assist them. These individuals are usually called facilitators because they ease or facilitate the processes undertaken by the team. A facilitator's primary job is to help the team and its leader discover answers for themselves without dictating an approach or an opinion.

In most organizations, it is an honor to be selected as either a team leader or a facilitator. The facilitator's role is more understated. His or her reward is esteem. Good facilitators are always in demand, since they have generally acquired the humanistic skills needed to develop and hone an organization. Good facilitators can make even marginal team leaders look polished and professional.

Role of the Facilitator

THE TEAM FACILITATOR ATTENDS team meetings, but is neither a team member nor leader. As a team "outsider," he or she can maintain an objective and neutral position. This neutrality is crucial for observing team progress, evaluating team behavior, and improving member interaction. The team facilitator also shows members how to use problem-solving tools and helps guide and focus the team's activities.

Facilitators rarely, if ever, run team meetings, handle administrative details, or carry out a team's between-meeting assignments. The facilitator works primarily before and after team meetings, conferring with the team leader. The team leader and team facilitator must meet frequently to assure the team's growth and proper focus. It is important, however, that facilitators occasionally "get their hands dirty," so that they can understand the business and manufacturing processes the team handles. Generally speaking, a good team facilitator should function equally well with either a team formed from a natural work group or one formed from multiple disciplines or departments.

In some companies, the person destined to be either the team leader or its facilitator may actually have the authority to create the team. This is generally only true when teams are formed to solve a particular set of problems.

It has been said that most of a team's work takes place while it is preparing to make a decision. The facilitator leads the team through the key processes needed to make sound decisions. He or she must address the tools required for analysis while focusing on group dynamics. The facilitator teaches team members how to collect data, examine and analyze it, and draw reasonable conclusions from it. At the same time, he or she must resolve any conflicts that might impede progress.

Managing and facilitating a team conflict somewhat. Autonomy should be encouraged, but the team cannot be allowed to proceed without control. The team leader and facilitator need to draw a fine line between empowerment to act independently and the appropriateness of actions taken.

Finally, the role of a facilitator does not end when the meetings adjourn. Effective facilitators further team cohesion between meetings by assuring communication on vital issues, project status, and new developments that may affect the functions of the team.

The Facilitator's Responsibilities

THE PRINCIPAL ACTIVITIES AND RESPONSIBILITIES of the team facilitator are:
- to focus his or her attention on the team problem-solving process, not the product under study. Be concerned more with the "how" of making decisions, rather than the "what";
- to remain as objective as possible. If he or she is a supervisor or manager, he or she must refrain from directing or coercing the team leader or members of the team. The team facilitator must disassociate his or her role from any other outside "boss/subordinate" relationship;
- to keep abreast of the principal problem-solving tools and techniques available for team use. Typically these include a strategy or method for attacking issues, such as the *Seven-Step Problem-Solving Approach* (to be discussed later) and various graphical and statistical data-gathering tools;
- to assist the team leader with structuring meetings, preparing agendas, and assigning tasks to team members. He or she should ensure that meetings are well planned and efficiently executed;
- to work between meetings on planning, decisions, and task structure. This will allow members to work efficiently on the issues when the meetings reconvene. The facilitator must be careful not to restrict the responsibilities or lessen the roles of team members, however;
- to act as a communication link with other teams, managers, supervisors, and outside consultants;

74

- to help team members become comfortable with statistics and proficient with tools and techniques;
- to help team members analyze information and draw proper conclusions from it. He or she should assist the team in its attempts to understand and relate to a problem properly;
- to encourage individuals to participate and develop skills within the group. He or she helps control difficult or dominating personalities within the group; and
- to interface with higher levels of management. The team usually needs a facilitator to help its members prepare presentations, reports, and requests to management or others.

If there is confusion or doubt about a specific technique or approach, the team facilitator should refer to an outside consultant or expert.

Facilitator Skills

THE IDEAL TEAM FACILITATOR HAS people, technical, and training skills; these are talents seldom found together in one individual, but they can be learned. Important traits in each area include:

- **people skills**–communication, listening, conflict resolution, feedback, counseling, meeting organization;
- **technical skills**–understanding how to gather and use data, project planning and organization, understanding problem-solving tools and techniques and their application to specific technical areas, understanding manufacturing processes, asking credible questions and get to the root of the issues; and
- **training skills**–teaching others how to use basic techniques, making effective presentations, showing others how to do the same.

Facilitator Training Topics

FACILITATORS MUST BE TRAINED in several principal areas. Outside consulting resources or qualified organization development staff within the company can help with this. Facilitator training is a good example of a "train the trainer" program; in a mature TQ environment, the team facilitator is also the team trainer. To accomplish this, at a minimum, prospective facilitators will need training in these areas:

- **organizing and conducting effective meetings**–setting the agenda, arranging for the facility and amenities, keeping the team membership on track, and generally assuring an efficient and productive meeting process;
- **problem-solving tools and techniques**–suggesting and teaching the application of technical tools, approaches, and techniques to the team and team leader as appropriate and timely (It is particularly important here that the facilitator have a suitable background and extensive first-hand problem-solving experience. The candidate must be able to do more than simply make a good presentation from a textbook or other prepared materials.);
- **group dynamics and conflict resolution**–understanding and practicing the techniques of developing group consensus and avoiding conflict. The facilitator must maintain consistent objectives throughout group interactions, focusing purely on the problem-solving process and not on personalities; and
- **effective listening**–objectively assessing the group and making suggestions for improving communication.

Facilitating Challenges

A TEAM FACILITATOR FACES MANY routine challenges. For this reason, it is important to put a great deal of thought into selecting one. Some of the challenges are:

- involving the entire team in problem-solving activities;
- dealing with specific individuals who have no interest, or who do not want to participate in the team's activities;
- maintaining enthusiasm and managing conflict;
- focusing on the issues at hand without trespassing on the leader's authority;

- dealing diplomatically with extroverted individuals who dominate the proceedings; and
- aligning company resources when appropriate.

Summary

UNDERSTANDING PROBLEM-SOLVING PROCESSES and choosing the methodology that best addresses the team's problems are not easy tasks. However, if a team has a strong, versatile leader and a well-trained, experienced facilitator, it will be much more effective.

CHAPTER 10

THE CONSULTANT'S ROLE

"Defining consultantcy is a bit like defining the upper class; every possible candidate draws the line just below himself."

– JOHN PEET, in *The Economist*

AN ORGANIZATION THAT WANTS to implement formal TQ and teambuilding should seek professional counsel. As pervasive as the quality ethic has become in this country, there are still painfully few great successes in TQM installations. An initiative installed because of a perceived need to "do something" is the most likely to fail. Often, a wise senior executive subscribes to an initiative because he or she believes the organization can increase productivity and competitiveness quickly and without overcoming the roadblocks others have experienced. This might be called the "this time it'll be different syndrome." Of even greater magnitude are those installations that have failed or withered caused by gradually diminishing management support. Even with a visionary executive providing unlimited support and resources, a hard, crushing failure is still possible.

Why TQM Fails

FAILURES CAN OCCUR FOR MANY reasons, but the four most prevalent are:
- the program of the day;
- failure in commitment;
- failure to consider people first; and
- solutions in search of problems.

The Program of the Day

MANY COMPANIES HAVE INSTALLED QUALITY and productivity initiatives with only mild degrees of success. These are the programs *du jour* or "the program of the day" and therefore are almost instantly held in low regard. Such programs are destined to fail.

Two good examples are Short Interval Scheduling (SIS) and Quality Circles. These initiatives had national "fad" appeal but little long-term success. The material they offered was generally well conceived, but many installations failed because the installing organization was not totally committed to them. They were also hindered by management's repeated failure to think strategically.

Failures in Commitment

TOTAL QUALITY IS A COMMITMENT, not a program. Commitment is not a matter of slogans, exhortations to do "good work," rewards and recognition, spending inordinate funds, holding rallies, or hosting civic events. It is a constant and continuous desire for continuous improvement in all enterprise operations.

A firm's senior management, including the CEO, chairman, and board of directors, must solidly commit to TQM. Occasionally, a single executive or a few visionary managers can drive a successful initiative at one business site, but the prognosis for keeping TQM alive as an institution is diminished. It is difficult to "spread the word" from the bottom or middle of an organization, particularly if there are no major quality and productivity successes during the first year or two of the initiative.

Commitment, once made by the top layer of management, is infectious; success will infect everyone, including the firm's suppliers and customers. Commitment makes everyone winners.

Once the initiative is up and running, the visionary executive or manager must direct his or her efforts toward public relations with the remaining skeptics. The visionary must keep the initiative alive and vital until everyone in the organization can see the payoffs.

Failure to Consider People First

MANY POPULAR COMPANY SLOGANS emphasize that people are the firm's most important resource. Beyond the rhetoric, people are crucial if TQM is to succeed. Ignoring the role of teams or short-shrifting an active teambuilding and training process will surely cause an initiative to fail, even with the most vital commitment.

Generally, American business pays little or no heed to the "people factor." New management tools are much more likely to be given more attention than job enrichment for personnel.

For example, many firms use statistical control techniques to define and improve manufacturing processes. Unfortunately, the emphasis is usually on the tools, rather than on the people using them. Many SPC (statistical process control) programs have been defeated because management did not provide teambuilding, facilitating, coaching, and counseling with SPC training.

Using statistical tools is a "scary" proposition for many production and office workers because they have not been trained in classical problem-solving techniques. The very word statistics is unnerving for many.

Solutions in Search of Problems

FREQUENTLY, MANAGEMENT BUYS INTO PROGRAMS that teach problem-solving techniques, only to realize later that the techniques have not been used effectively, if at all. Employees trained in the use of statistical process control charts, for example, must be guided, coached and counseled if they are to observe process problems and know when to apply controls. Quite often employees are trained and then ordered to "go solve problems." Management must realize that all training must be complemented with assistance in real-world applications.

In the early years of TQ, tools and techniques were emphasized, sampling and process control charts in particular. Oddly enough, this was diametrically opposed to the earlier Quality Circles era, when work groups were given resources, time, and guidance, but little technical or problem-solving training. A successful TQM initiative must not only contain all elements of training and facilitation, but must also focus on the individual employee and the team's ability to direct these newfound tools in the workplace.

An employee training program is not TQM. SPC is not TQM. Group meetings are not TQM. Teams are not "solutions in search of a problem." TQ is the focused, committed, and directed use of employees and their inherent skills to improve the enterprise's quality and productivity process constantly.

Consultants, Trainers, and Facilitators

AFTER THE DECISION TO INITIATE A TQ or teambuilding initiative is made, the visionary executive may be contacted by consulting and training firms that offer a wide variety of services. It is important for the contracting company to examine closely the skills, successes, and capabilities of such TQ companies.

First, decide that you need a consultant, not a trainer or a facilitator. A good consultant performs all these functions, but trainers are rarely good consultants and facilitators. Companies that deal exclusively in training perform excellent services, but with narrow vision. The typical trainer is usually skilled in his or her topic, but limited in those skills needed to apply techniques in the real world. Industrial training is similar to classroom teaching at a high school or university level. Many excellent teachers, skilled at presentation, lack business experience. A visionary executive or the TQ steering committee should rigorously review the credentials of companies or individuals offering training services to verify their abilities to facilitate use of techniques. They must verify that these service providers know how to use and facilitate these techniques at the workplace. If contracting a training firm is under consideration, they should consider seeking purchasing advice from a consultant not associated with the firm. They also must check client references thoroughly.

Facilitators should be selected from the company staff and trained appropriately. TQM is a long-term commitment made by a company's management. As such, it means a continuing investment of time and money. Also, the nature of tasks within the installation will change gradually. A consultant can shift roles during the implementation, to respond to the needs of the moment.

Initially, a TQM installation requires planning, publicity, public relations, communication, and establishing a vision, a mission, values, principles, and objectives. Teams are then formed and trained in technical problem-solving approaches and the group dynamics of teambuilding. Facilitators and team leaders also must receive training tailored to their roles. When the teams have been built, the tools that manage the manufacturing and business process should be applied seriously and with an eye to achieving results.

A consultant can direct, manage, and counsel the company as it enters and completes each phase of the process. A good consultant acts as the "control center" for a multitude of activities, including planning, training, customer and vendor interfacing, corporate interacting, and managing the process.

Shopping for a Consultant

THERE ARE A FEW KEY PARAMETERS for "shopping" for a TQ initiative consultant:
- qualifications and realistic planning. A potential supplier should project realistically the duration and benefits of contracted services. A draft of a mini initiative "game plan" based on earlier successful installation should be created during the first meetings with the consultant;
- commitment, flexibility, and follow-through. The consultant must commit his or her time and estimate the number of visits necessary for continuous consultation, support, and address of contingency issues. The consultant should be able to work with all employees at any time (day or night) during the implementation process. He or she should feel equally at ease

with senior executives and the lowest job groups. The consultant must be able to establish rapport with employees so that they believe they can make a change; and

• demonstrated quality. The contractor should serve as the very model of quality services. He or she should demonstrate continuous improvement and the ability to learn even more from experience. Consultants and trainers both should demonstrate how they make changes to their own routines. Above all, they should be moderately humble and self-effacing, while using humor to ease business problems.

Consulting Firm Hierarchies

CONSULTANTS ARE BUSINESSMEN AND WOMEN. As such, their profit and survival motives are as strong as any business interest. In large consulting firms, there are established hierarchies and mini-bureaucracies that are tied to the business lifeblood, the "billable day" (or "billable hour"). Professionals sell talent by the hour, and consultants are no exception.

Like other enterprises, consulting operations also carry overhead expenses and must amortize them. The larger the firm, the greater the overhead, and, presumably, the greater the billable rate.

There are several ways to control cost, but the most significant is to use the lowest grade professional labor that can accomplish the task at hand. In a typical consulting proposal, there may be three or more labor grades applied to the tasks. At the lowest level, the firm may employ "associate" or "junior" consultants. Typically, these are young individuals with minimal business experience, but good academic credentials. In a medical analogy, these are the interns and first-year residents who perform daily patient care and routine diagnostic tasks.

Next in the hierarchy is the consultant, typically a seasoned professional with some years of experience in the business or in industry. He or she directs junior colleagues, sifts and allocates activities, and deals with the more complex items. The consultant is akin to a staff physician.

A senior consultant is an insightful and experienced professional. He or she may have developed the firm's original consulting proposal. He or she is a senior work director for the project, directing, controlling, and disbursing funds, operations reports, presentations and program reviews for the client. A senior consultant may also be a partner in the consulting firm. In the medical analogy, he or she is the specialist or chief of service or staff.

When dealing with a large firm, the client may see three or four (or more) individuals over the span of the contract. He or she will also be billed at a rate computed by allocating three or more skill levels into the tasks. The billable day rate, for example, may be based on an average of 15 percent project management, 30 percent associate-level work, and 55 percent consultant-level work, plus a pro-rata share of overhead and general and administrative expenses.

The visionary executive seeking TQ and teambuilding consulting services is advised to consider small firms or single-person contractors first. The cash outlay per billable day will generally be substantially less, the communication links better, and project management less bureaucratic and more effective. Furthermore, teambuilding is best served by minimizing personalities; the fewer "outsiders" coming and going, the better. Large firms, of course, will argue that their experience base is much larger with greater resources. Greater experience is certainly worthwhile, but it may not be a substantial asset if too many people and personalities are involved. The TQM battle plan needs a "general"course, will argue that their experience base is much larger with greater resources. Greater experience is certainly

The division of labor in a small consulting firm is between the principal (i.e., the "project manager") and the "trainer," if indeed they are not the same person. From the contracting company's standpoint, it is substantially easier to communicate with one or two well-focused individuals than a hierarchy of "troops." Further, individuals in the business will be more comfortable with only one or a few familiar faces during the many months of planning, training, and execution.

The Consultant's Role

GIVEN THE MANY OPPORTUNITIES for initiative failure, what contribution can a consultant make? Secondly, how long should it be before the business and the consultant see a vital and successful initiative?

85

The Consultant's Contributions

FIRST AND FOREMOST, THE OUTSIDE consultant brings experience. He or she has implemented TQ in other firms. This is a valuable asset. The experienced consultant has seen successes and failures and has (one hopes) cataloged the events and corresponding information. A consultant helps prevent the "reinventing the wheel" syndrome.

The consultant is a trained facilitator. He or she can plan, organize, and help work groups become fully functional teams. He or she knows how to avoid an imbalance between emphasis on training and tools while building effective teams from work groups.

The consultant is an experienced manager. He or she has worked with all organizational levels, developed plans and strategies, coached and counseled employees, and directed technical projects. The consultant knows how to maximize the resources given to the TQM project and how to sell it to all levels.

The consultant is versed in current tools and techniques. A good consultant, like a physician or surgeon, remains technically proficient by keeping abreast of developments in the field. He or she is active in professional societies, community and civic groups, and educational institutions. Frequently, he or she writes for technical or business journals, or may even write textbooks. A good consultant refines tools and techniques based on experience, so that any given problem-solving approach is tempered and made more effective.

The consultant is an icon in the workplace, carrying a mystique that helps expedite the project. Employees initially tend to regard the consultant with respect (and a good dose of suspicion) for a while. Good consultants then become entrenched in the organization, as advisers and wise counselors. They are only concerned with the TQ initiative, not "office politics," staff personal problems, or other priorities. A consultant must be good-natured and willing to admit failures or shortcomings. He or she stands beside and behind the TQ visionaries, offering any skill appropriate to selling and sustaining the initiative.

The consultant can objectively assess progress. Most individuals in a paid consulting role respect the responsibilities their profession places on them. Foremost is the obligation to remain objective and honest in all client dealings. Though aware of internal company stresses and organizational strains, the professional consultant maintains objectivity toward the tasks at hand. By focusing on the initiative, he or she provides rare and valuable insight to the installation. The consultant's professional objectivity also allows him or her frequent access to information of an "institutional" nature that may assist with the case at hand. Without breaching confidences, a consultant can gather useful information that may otherwise evade visionary executives.

Duration of the Consulting Assignment

IT CAN BE DIFFICULT TO ASSESS the duration and cost of TQ and teambuilding initiatives. Clearly, continuous improvement and TQM are lifelong commitments that must be made by the enterprise; it is also clear that a functioning, vital, and successful system cannot be established within a single business year. Consequently, the visionary executive or manager must, as part of the commitment-building public relations process, gain support for funding and other resources for a multi-year period. The organization must also be prepared for no payback in the current year, a difficult concept for most American businesses to absorb.

Installing TQM takes from two to five years in many cases. Experience indicates that many companies are "weaned" from outside assistance after two to three years, followed by occasional outside "audits" that verify the initiative's integrity.

The consultant's role declines as management and teams mature and begin managing their own activities. In a medium-sized manufacturing operation, on-site consulting time should decline in a prescribed manner over a two or three year period, reaching the "audit" stage in the third or fourth year. In the first year, the consultant may be on-site 60 or 70 percent of available work time. During the second year, that may decline to 30 to 40 percent; and in the third year become 20 percent. Over a three-year period, the consultant may be on the business premises for the equivalent of a full year, in addition to time spent at the home office.

The pragmatic company exercises a prudent consultant selection process and commits resources for the long haul. The business buys, nominally, perhaps a year's worth of consulting, spread over a two to four year period. The investment is substantial, but the returns can be astounding.

The best outcome for any consultant is to complete the TQM initiative so effectively that he or she "works him or herself out of a job." In a monumentally successful installation (Xerox, Ford, and Federal Express are some excellent examples), the initiative is so well received that the company spends substantial additional resources to "spread the word" to other locations, divisions, vendors, and customers. After Xerox was presented the Malcolm Baldrige National Quality Award, untold company funds and consulting time were spent publicizing the event. They also used it as a sales and marketing tool.

When The Consultant Leaves

CONSULTING ASSIGNMENTS ARE FINITE. When a project has ended, it is generally obvious. Line-item activities diminish, the consultant is on-site much less often, and working groups have significantly less calls for outside assistance. In addition, the consultant's mystique should have worn thin. No longer the icon, the outsider is now a familiar fixture at the business.

Before the consultant's last visit in the installation phase (perhaps in the third year of activity), arrangements must be made to assure continuity. At this point, the business managers need to make a decision. If the TQ initiative is succeeding, progressing, and contributing to the firm's success, then an arrangement must be made either to assume future training and audit tasks in-house or to contract the same with the consultant's company.

The company also may wish to structure a checklist for ongoing audits. This should be done collectively by the steering committee, teams, and consulting staff.

In any case, the company should establish a telephone "hot line" to the consultant and the consultant should be available for public relations efforts and presentations on behalf of the company's business.

Alternatives to Consulting

THIS CHAPTER CANNOT BE CLOSED without a brief discussion of the alternatives to purchasing outside consulting services for TQM installation. If the visionary company and its management choose to pursue a path of establishing internal expertise, they must commit to an earnest employee selection and training process. Initially, a minimum of two, and preferably three, senior personnel must be selected for TQM familiarization and formal training. A single candidate is not advised, since he or she may leave the firm or otherwise become unable to continue the installation. The persons selected must be experienced, reasonably skilled in human relations, and close to the median age of the employee population at large. These parameters are important, for they establish capability and forge respect. Some seniority is absolutely necessary to command respect with older, more senior employee groups.

The candidates must then embark on an intense training agenda. This ranges from classroom and seminar training in TQM principles to field trips to several successful companies, preferably in similar businesses. Substantial investment of time, materials, and outside resources is paramount in bringing the selected employees "up to speed" on TQ and team-building topics and establishing their facilitation skills. Essentially, the training process introduces topics that will be intensely studied and practiced before they are used in the field by senior and respected employees. These topics include applying statistical process control techniques. For this, a company may choose to use an outside SPC trainer and purchase off-the-shelf training materials. This takes less time than developing totally new skills in the candidates.

Overall, the process of establishing an internal TQM capability is not one to be taken lightly. It means a substantial commitment and absolute dedication to succeeding. If part of the internal consultant's role will be to "spread the word" over many company locations or divisions, then the investment may be worthwhile. Otherwise, make one or more selections from the many excellent consultants available in the field. You will not be disappointed.

CHAPTER 11

THE PROBLEM–SOLVING PROCESS

"I hope we are over our belief that if you define a problem you don't have to do any work."

– PETER DRUCKER

MOST ENGINEERS, MANAGERS, AND PROFESSIONALS have the educational and working backgrounds to understand a scientific approach to solving problems. Many non-professional and plant personnel, however, do not. That is why it is so important that facilitators, team leaders, and team members be familiar with the generalized process of structuring and solving a problem. This should be done before teaching specific tools and techniques, and certainly before using any statistical processes.

To use any problem-solving approach, a team must be able observe, question, record, analyze, reason, and synthesize. These are defined as follows:

observing–taking an inventory of the activity being considered; determining the what, when, where, how, and who of each part of the situation;

questioning–asking those individuals and groups who can provide facts intelligent questions about the process that cannot be obtained by direct observation;

recording–documenting in a logical, factual, and systematic manner;

analyzing–breaking data and information down into logical and clearly-understood areas to document cause and effect;

reasoning–determining the objective, problem, logical approaches, and solution; and

synthesizing–using creativity to create alternative solutions.

The Seven-Step Approach

THE SEVEN-STEP APPROACH IS A POPULAR and workable approach to problem-solving. The team and team leader apply the steps assisted by the team facilitator and, if necessary, an outside consultant. It is a logical and rational approach to defining and solving any anomalous situation that can be applied by any group or individual at any time.

This and similar approaches may also be called the "scientific approach" to problem-solving. It is the basis of most problem-solving techniques, programs, or systems that have been described or taught publicly or privately. This includes the work simplification approach, which was introduced in the 1930s, and the classic methods engineering approach pioneered by General Motors Corporation. It is also the basis for value analysis and value engineering techniques that deal with providing the most functional product for the least cost (value).

The seven steps of the process are as follows:

Step 1–Determine the Problem and Objective. A team must decide on an exact definition of the problem. Following this, the exact objective should be determined. A study cannot be undertaken without an objective in mind; the objective cannot be accomplished if the problem is not understood.

Sometimes it may be difficult to determine which problems deserve priority; also, many times problems are so complex and interwoven that simply determining the direction to take can seem to be a monumental task.

Effective tools and techniques that can be used in this step include brainstorming, nominal group techniques, Pareto analysis, flow charts, and histograms. The specific application rules for all techniques are detailed in the next chapter.

Step 2–Study Conditions. Once the problem is identified and the objectives stated, conditions surrounding the situation should be examined. This step provides a complete understanding of the problem, how its many factors interact, and its possible causes and effects. The team and its leader should ask questions and then use logic, common sense, and proven techniques to determine cause and effect. The team may choose to ask questions in the following format:

In this situation (that we as a team agree is a problem):
What is being done? Why is it being done at all?
When is it being done? Why is it being done at that time?
Where is it being done? Why is it being done at that place?
How is it being done? Why is it being done by that method?
Who does it? Why is it being done by that person?

The team should gather pertinent facts about the processes involved and try to determine their interactions. From these facts, the team can most likely find the probable cause of the existing problem condition.

Basic tools and techniques that can be applied in this step include cause-and-effect analysis, flow charts, run charts, scatter diagrams, and histograms.

Step 3—Develop Possible Solutions. The team is now in the position to plan the solution to the problem or issue. The first factor to consider is the objective, since alternate solutions may have to satisfy what the team originally outlined as important considerations. For example, if the objective includes the statement "with minimum expense," purchasing special tools or automated equipment may be out of the question. If the objective states that the problem must be resolved "within six weeks," other alternatives may be ruled out.

Regardless of the range of alternatives, consideration should be given first and foremost to those approaches that garner greatest value; in other words, how can the function be accomplished at the least cost? This is a time to use brainstorming. Other tools that can help include nominal group techniques and flow charts.

Step 4—Evaluate Possible Solutions. Evaluating various alternatives involves considering a number of factors. These include cost, quality, safety, product design, material and process specifications, equipment and facilities, manpower, tooling, plant layout, and other items.

The team should attempt to evaluate all solutions completely, noting their advantages and disadvantages. Otherwise, it will be difficult to make an informed comparison. With consensus, the team can proceed toward a recommended action.

Some techniques that can be used in this step are: brainstorming, nominal group techniques, and flow charts.

Step 5—Recommend Action. Developing and evaluating alternatives for action eventually brings the team to a point where recommendations must be made to management. The team's proposal, formal or informal, should always include at least two factors:

1. a list of the proposal's benefits (in quality, safety, schedule, or cost); and

2. the costs of implementing the suggested alternative. In other words, what will be the net benefit if the team's suggestion is followed?

The presentation may be formal or informal, depending on the magnitude and the preferences of the team, steering committee, and cognizant management.

Step 6—Follow Up. Upon approval of the approach, the team must implement its plan and monitor the process involved to assure that change is made and that the solution is the right one. The team leader should coordinate with the support and technical groups involved to implement the suggested change. The action should be maintained on the team's action register for the duration of implementation and prove-out, and each week the project's status should be discussed in a regular team meeting.

Step 7—Check Results. Sometimes the best solutions proposed by a team may not function exactly as planned; therefore, it is usually prudent to include a trial period or test run. In addition to allowing the team to check the approach for effectiveness, a test period also allows verification of the benefits and costs associated with installing the solution.

The team should also be sure that the original objectives have been accomplished and that the solution has not created additional problems somewhere else.

If the team is satisfied with the approach, if benefits have occurred as predicted, and if the revised process is stable, then the item may be removed from the team's action register.

Some tools that can be used in this step are: run charts, scatter diagrams, histograms, and control charts.

Whether or not these steps are formally documented, they do take place in the order listed when the technique is used successfully. In small-scale, short-duration efforts, some steps might appear to have been omitted; in fact, all steps are usually done, but sometimes with little formality or recognition of what is happening in the problem-solving process.

After a while, the team will become comfortable with the seven steps of problem-solving, using tools and techniques, and handling multiple issues or problems concurrently. Undoubtedly, certain issues or problems will be difficult and the team may not be able to handle them immediately. Other problems may have no immediate solution, despite appearing to be simple on the surface. However, if the team is firmly committed to working through these with the seven-step process, even these situations may be settled.

CHAPTER 12

PROBLEM–SOLVING TOOLS

"A single idea, if it is right, saves us the labor of an infinity of experiences."

– JACQUES MARITAIN

THERE ARE MANY EASY-TO-USE AND readily available tools and techniques that teams in a TQ environment may use. Some are statistical in nature, such as histograms, scatter diagrams, and control charts; others are described as "management" tools and techniques. In the management "tool kit" are such items as brainstorming, Pareto analysis, and nominal group techniques.

This chapter describes the basic tools and techniques of quality management, including both the technical and management tools. Each discussion provides a total description of the approach (**what** and **how?**) and the conditions under which it is normally used (**why** and **when?**). Further, the information indicates responsibility for its facilitation and use (**who?**). A short discussion of advantages and disadvantages is included (PROS AND CONS), as well as tips on usage (*Hints*).

Brainstorming

What? Brainstorming is a proven technique that generates as many ideas as possible quickly. It is an exciting technique because it offers individuals and groups a chance to exercise freewheeling creativity while having fun. Furthermore, brainstorming is productive because group members can build on the ideas of others as the process continues.

The two common methods of brainstorming are referred to as "structured" (also called "sequenced"), and "unstructured" (also called "unsequenced"). In the structured method, team members share their ideas in sequence around the table, until all ideas have been listed; in the unstructured method, members of the team contribute ideas randomly.

How? The team leader prepares a written problem statement to help focus the team's attention on the established goal.

After all team members agree on and understand the nature of the problem, they volunteer ideas. The team leader lists these on a chalkboard or flip chart for all to see. This continues until all members have exhausted their thoughts or "pass" to the next individual around the table. In general, the rules include the following:

- there should be no initial criticism of any idea;
- evaluation comes later; "freewheeling" is welcomed. Ideas can be toned down later; all thoughts should be encouraged. The more ideas there are, the greater the likelihood of good ones;
- "hitchhiking" or "piggybacking" is encouraged. Build on the ideas of others;
- everyone must participate for brainstorming to be effective. Interaction is a necessity; and
- the team leader must record every idea, even the "wild" ones.

After the possibilities are exhausted, the team leader should poll the group to identify ideas that can be combined or eliminated because they duplicate another. In this process, the individual that originally provided an idea must agree to its elimination. There is still no criticism or evaluation at this stage.

After narrowing the list, the leader then must lead the group to consensus by ranking the ideas according to value and usefulness. This can be done by a show of hands on each idea, or asking each team member to list his or her "top three" or "top five" in order. The team leader is the vote keeper and leader of discussion. When the consensus is reached, the leader then opens the floor for critical discussion of each item and eventually strives for consensus on the single best (or two best) approach(es). Brainstorming usually yields fresh and new ideas, as well as thoughts that may not be obvious outside the group.

Why? To assist a team in reaching agreement on a problem, topic, or plan of action.

When? Brainstorming is used when the team needs many thoughts or ideas about problems or causes, or the members must identify obstacles to progress.

When used properly, brainstorming improves group communications, fosters teamwork, and helps make solving problems more fun and interesting for group members. It is a powerful technique that is used throughout the problem-solving process, but is most commonly applied to steps 1, 3, and 4 of the Seven-Step Approach discussed in Chapter 11.

Who? The team leader, team, and facilitator.

PROS AND CONS. Brainstorming generates many ideas in a short time. It is also "fun" and encourages group cohesion. Its very nature may discourage some people from participating, however, particularly if they are quiet and reserved when in a group setting. Also, some team members tend to pre-judge or criticize ideas and others may not want to participate. The team leader and facilitator must encourage freewheeling and discourage criticism so that all members have an opportunity to contribute to the process.

Hints. For brainstorming to be effective, the team must first agree on the method it will use, who will record ideas, and what the order of discussion is.

They must also decide which rules to follow during the brainstorming sessions. Team members should be encouraged to be creative and to speak up. In the initial idea listing phase, no thought is too ridiculous. Someone's "wild idea" may just work or it may cause someone else to suggest another related idea that is more practical. The team leader should foster a relaxed, fun atmosphere. Humor boosts creativity, but criticism can kill it. It is very important to keep criticism and prejudice out of the brainstorming session. The "structured" form of brainstorming should be used if team members are not totally comfortable in the setting or with each other.

If a problem is particularly complex or difficult, it often helps to allow an incubation period. In these cases, the brainstorming session should be started at one meeting and completed the next. Even after the session is over, team members should be encouraged to suggest new ideas at any time. They can always be added to the list and evaluated along with the others.

Nominal Group Techniques (NGT)

What? Nominal group techniques (NGT) are relatively new and effective creativity techniques. Like brainstorming, they are used for developing ideas. Unlike brainstorming, the approach is formal and structured. A qualified leader or facilitator must lead it.

NGT is a simple and controlled method. If there are individuals who tend to dominate conversation in the group, NGT equalizes the opportunities for discussion, since initial contributions are not spoken. Because of the relative formality, it does not generally create as many ideas as brainstorming, nor as many that can be "piggy-backed" onto others. NGT assumes agreement, or consensus, of a group on a given set of issues or topics.

How? The team leader prepares a written problem statement so that the team may focus on the established goal.

After all team members agree on and understand the problem, each team member lists ideas on a piece of paper. Individuals write every thought or idea until they have exhausted their imaginations. As the team leader sees each member complete a list, he or she will announce "a few minutes remain" so that others will finish promptly. The team leader then asks each member in turn to provide one item that the leader may list on a chalkboard or flip chart. The ideas given by the group are not necessarily in any order. Each member adds an idea until they are exhausted and must "pass" to the next. This procedure continues until all the ideas are listed.

In the next step, the team leader asks the members to list, on paper, their "top choice(s)." This may be one idea, the "top three," "top five," or any logical number. The members review the composite group list and choose favorite ideas from the long list so that it eventually becomes a "short list." The short list is then refined; the end result should be consensus on the "best" ideas. The voting could be done with a show of hands or verbally, but this might discourage further participation. The general rules of the NGT process are similar to brainstorming.

Why? To assist a team in reaching agreement on a problem, topic, or plan of action.

When? NGT may be used when the team must reach consensus but may not be totally comfortable with brainstorming. It is commonly applied in steps 1, 3, and 4 of the Seven-Step Approach. However, if the team is comfortable with it, NGT may be used throughout the process of defining and solving a problem, at any time creativity is needed, or whenever consensus is required.

Who? The team leader, team, and facilitator.

PROS AND CONS. NGT is used to generate ideas in a short time. Because it is a more formal and structured technique, it is not usually as much "fun" as unstructured brainstorming. Because there is no oral humor, sometimes fewer ideas are generated, particularly "wild" ones.

However, since it uses written lists, more members may feel comfortable participating; judgment and criticism are not factors.

Hints. The team leader is responsible for moving the NGT process along. In general, the process of listing ideas should not take more than 15 to 20 minutes; this includes combining and eliminating overlapping ideas. Overall, the group should arrive at the "top three" or "top five" easily within a half hour. If desired, the written approach may be used in each round of the procedure, up to and including written ballots on the final consensus.

Since NGT usually involves writing, the team leader should assure that paper or note pads and pencils are provided. As each individual brings an idea forward, he or she should cross it out. When each individual's ideas are exhausted, they should say "pass" and defer to the next. If a new thought comes up, they should, however, add it to the list on their next turn.

Secret ballots generally are not recommended; however, if they are used, the group should agree to them before they start the exercise. If ideas are expected to be totally "wild" or "off the wall," the team leader may collect the member's papers and post them, without verbal comment by anyone in the group. That way, each idea is anonymous. In any case, the team leader should always foster a relaxed, fun atmosphere, limiting criticism and pre-judgment until an appropriate time in the process.

As with brainstorming, it may be useful to allow an incubation period. Let team members sleep on it. In these cases, the NGT session should be started at one meeting and completed the next. A logical stopping point may be when all ideas have been initially listed; the leader may wish the team to consider the selection of their "top three" or "top five" priorities carefully. After any session, team members should still be encouraged to add new ideas at any time. If there is a consensus on the value of the new thought, it may be added to the initial list and priorities reevaluated.

Cause-and Effect Analysis

What? After the team has identified an important problem, members must then ask "what are some of the possible causes?" Cause-and-effect analysis is a powerful tool often used to determine the cause(s) of an "effect" (the problem itself).

As in brainstorming, asking the question, "what are some of the possible causes?" often creates an abundance of ideas. Cause-and-effect analysis helps your team focus on causes they feel are related to the previously defined problem. It also utilizes a technique that will help your team members broaden the span of their creative ideas.

Cause-and-effect analysis was developed by Dr. Kaoru Ishikawa of Tokyo University. For this reason, it is sometimes referred to as an Ishikawa Diagram. The shape of the diagram brought about its more common name, *fishbone diagram.* The diagram resembles a fishbone, with the problem or defect—the "effect"—shown at the right of the diagram (or "head" of the fish). The "ribs" or "bones" growing from the center are the possible causes of the problem at hand. The chart can help identify how many varied and separate causes might interact to give the end effect.

How? A cause-and-effect analysis usually means examining four areas. These are usually shown as the **Four Ms:** manpower (or people), machines, methods, and materials. In manufacturing, almost all reasons for a problem's existence can be traced back to one of these areas. They may be used as the starting point for drawing the "bones" of the diagram. Figure 12.1 shows a cause-and-effect analysis done for a problem in fork lift truck availability and "uptime" in a manufacturing plant. In the example, many possible reasons for unavailability have been listed by a team of operators. Note that the Four Ms support many sub-branches that are individually addressed and evaluated as potential parts of the problem.

In areas other than manufacturing, the Four Ms may vary. For example, in a hospital setting, the major factors may be equipment, staffing, supplies, and procedures. In city government, it might be systems, organization, procedures, and equipment. Selecting the diagram's major branches is the responsibility of the team. If necessary, it may be changed later.

The diagram lists the effect and then traces the causes with a system of branching lines. Team members broaden the base of their creative thinking by suggesting categories. Cause-and-effect diagramming is usually drawn horizontally, on a chalkboard or large flip chart. The record should be permanent, so chalkboards may not be the best approach. As the diagram becomes more complex, it may be necessary to add new sections of paper and tape the result to a wall.

Cause-and-effect analysis is done in four major steps: **problem definition, major cause selection** ("bones" in the diagram), **speculation,** and **selection of most likely solutions.** The process is concluded with appropriate actions and a follow-up that determines whether the solution(s) are effective. The process may be repeated many times to select and "cure" problems correctly in a single diagram.

First, the team must clearly define the problem and verify that all team members understand the definition. Write the problem on the right-hand

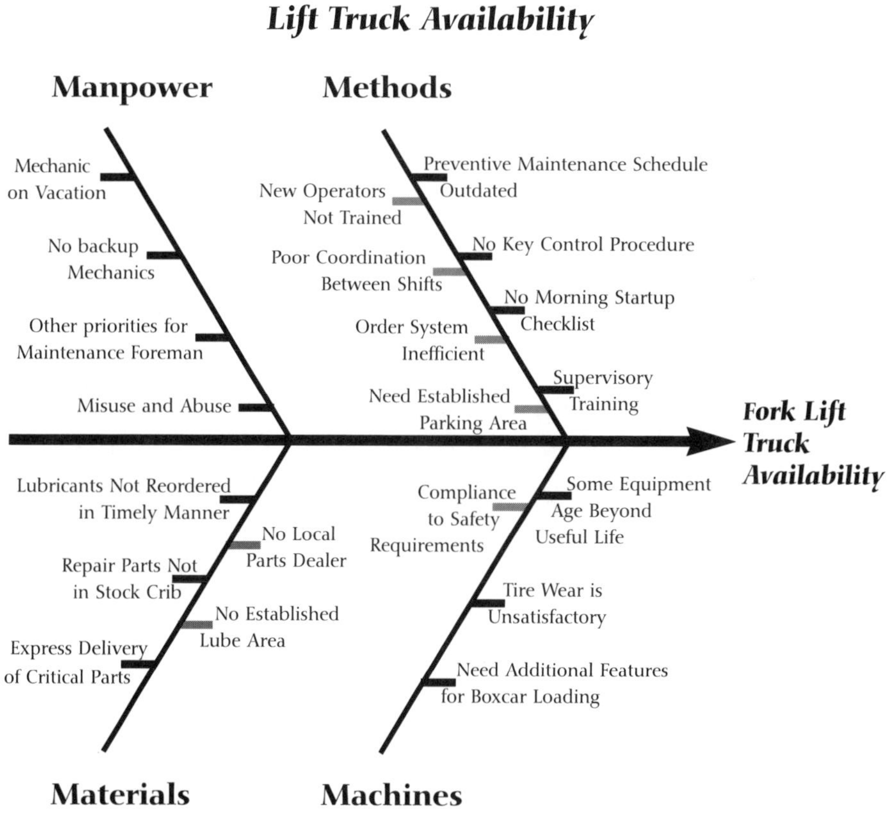

Lift Truck Availability

Manpower

Mechanic on Vacation

No backup Mechanics

Other priorities for Maintenance Foreman

Misuse and Abuse

Lubricants Not Reordered in Timely Manner

Repair Parts Not in Stock Crib

Express Delivery of Critical Parts

No Local Parts Dealer

No Established Lube Area

Methods

New Operators Not Trained

Poor Coordination Between Shifts

Order System Inefficient

Need Established Parking Area

Preventive Maintenance Schedule Outdated

No Key Control Procedure

No Morning Startup Checklist

Supervisory Training

Compliance to Safety Requirements

Some Equipment Age Beyond Useful Life

Tire Wear is Unsatisfactory

Need Additional Features for Boxcar Loading

Fork Lift Truck Availability

Materials   **Machines**

Figure 12.1. Cause and Effect Analysis

103

side of the flip chart paper and draw a box around it. This is called the effect. Draw a process arrow leading into the box. It represents the causes' direction of influence.

Second, decide the major categories. The Four Ms may be appropriate, but it is more important to use words that mean something to the team members.

Third, use brainstorming or NGT to generate ideas about possible causes. When an idea is suggested, write it in the most appropriate category. Encourage team members to identify both a possible cause and the category to which it belongs. Continue the process until as many probable causes have been identified as possible. (The more probable causes your team identifies, the greater the probability that you will uncover the true cause.) Ask the members to review the diagram and think about the possible impact of each cause.

Finally, the team should select the most likely cause(s). The group should discuss their opinions. The leader should encourage the group to look for any correlations between the problem and the causes. Select a few causes that the team feels should be investigated further. No ideas should be discarded. Most teams can reach a consensus, although voting for "the top three" is another widely used approach. Once the selections are made, the leader should circle the team's top choices on the chart.

After completing the four major steps in selection, the team should devise a test or study that either proves or disproves the circled causes. Make sure all team members understand and support this step. Also make sure that team members understand the investigative task and when it should be completed.

Sometimes the causes selected for investigation turn out not to be the true cause of the problem. When this occurs, the leader should direct the team back to the cause-and-effect diagram to search for other likely causes.

Why? To identify possible causes of a problem and start an investigative process to determine the most likely cause.

When? Cause-and-effect analysis helps a team visualize the factors influencing a particular problem. It is most useful in Step 2 of the Seven-Step Approach, after the team has used brainstorming, NGT, and Pareto analysis.

Who? The team leader, team, and facilitator. People outside the team or technical specialists may also be included in the exercise or add comments after the initial session.

PROS AND CONS. Because of its visual nature and the group interaction needed to list and post possible causes, the cause-and-effect method is frequently used as a problem analysis tool. It is structured, easily used, and easily understood. The odds that it will be successful are favorable.

Some team members may become impatient during the process. They may wish to omit listing all possible causes and proceed to their own ideas about the "real cause." The team leader must not to allow individuals to jump to conclusions without group consensus, however.

Hints. To minimize frustration, the team leader should keep the discussion confined to an area the team can control. Further, the possible causes should be listed as concisely as possible.

Many teams post the cause-and-effect analysis diagram where those who are not team members can add their ideas. These ideas can be written directly on the chart or attached to the chart on note paper or "Post-It" notes. Not only does this technique provide additional ideas, but it often creates a wider awareness of the problem. This can lead to a solution without direct team action.

Pareto Analysis

What? A Pareto analysis is used to count and display a number of defects or problems, to determine which have the greatest impact on operations or improvement. The information is displayed as bars or lines of varying length on a chart. The chart is called a Pareto and quickly and clearly shows which causes are responsible for a disproportionate number of results. It is easy to construct and easy to understand. The chart can also be useful for identifying points in the production process at which defects of certain types are most likely to occur.

Pareto analysis is named for the nineteenth-century Italian economist Vilfredo Pareto. He speculated that 20 percent of Italy's population controlled 80 percent of its wealth. Others have applied his speculations to more subjects and concluded that about 80 percent of all effects can be traced to about 20 percent of all causes; conversely, the remaining 80 percent of causes account for only about 20 percent of the effects.

How? After an area for study has been selected, a Pareto chart can be prepared to investigate what particular problems cause the greatest effect. Data for a Pareto analysis can be obtained from several sources, including maintenance records, quality and inspection reports, sampling, and observing of factory operations.

In the examples shown in figures 12.2 and 12.3, the number of defects is shown on the vertical axis, while types of defects appear on the horizontal axis. The causes contributing the greatest number of defects are posted from the left to the right. When the chart is completed, it is easy to select those problems that have the greatest effects. Generally, the first few causes listed from left to right account for about 80 percent (plus or minus) of all effects.

Why? To rank and prioritize problems or areas that concern the team.

When? Pareto charting is used to maximize improvement efforts by attacking the few causes responsible for the most problems. Pareto charts help identify the relatively few categories of causes that account for most

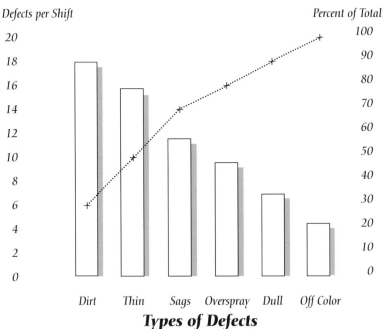

Types of Defects

Figure 12.2. Pareto Chart, Paint Department Problems

problems. Therefore, it is most useful in Step 1 of the Seven-Step Approach.

Who? The team leader, team, and facilitator. The technique can also be used by individuals alone.

Pros and Cons. The Pareto technique is simple to use and understand. If data is gathered and used properly, there will be very little argument regarding the priorities for problem-solving.

One misleading factor may be the relative cost associated with each effect on the chart. For example, if a problem that occurs infrequently has high costs associated with failure, the team may wish to rank effects by cost, not frequency.

Hints. Always draw bars or lines on the chart from the left, starting with the item of the largest magnitude. Percentages may also be noted from left to right across the chart.

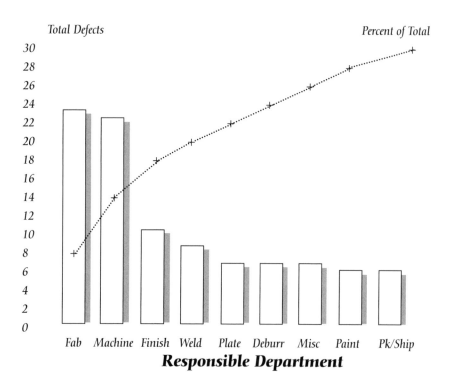

Figure 12-3 Pareto Chart, Defects by Department

It should be noted that the most frequent or most expensive single problems are not necessarily the most important overall. When the major problems (those contributing to the "80 percent") are fixed, the team should review the situation to see which "new" causes are now high priority.

Flow Charts

What? The flow chart, often called a process flow chart and sometimes an input–output chart, uses standardized symbols to represent sequential steps of a process or procedure. It describes an unfamiliar series of steps so that a team may understand the sequence of events and how these process steps relate to each other.

How? Flow charts use symbols to refer to activities in the flow of a process. Which symbols are used is generally not as important as a clear description of the sequence. Flow charts can also be used to design improved work processes because they can illustrate how things should happen.

A popular symbol set is that of the ASME (American Society of Mechanical Engineers). It features five basic symbol shapes. A circle means an operation, a square means an inspection point, a D–shaped symbol means delay, an arrow means movement, and an inverted triangle means a storage point. Rectangular boxes may be used as explanatory labels. There are a few other symbol conventions, but these few are usually sufficient to detail a process. Figure 12.4 shows a simple flow chart that uses the ASME symbols.

Some teams use a system of flow chart symbols called systems flow symbols. These generally consist of the decision "diamond" shape, oval, and rectangular or square shapes, and connecting lines. Figure 12.5 shows a flow chart with these system symbol conventions. This system also incorporates symbols for various computer-based events, such as report generation and on–line file storage of data.

Why? To identify all steps of a process or procedure pictorially so that team members and others may easily understand it.

When? Because flow charts help a team visualize the many and some-times complex steps of a process, a flow chart can be used to define a process before specific problem–solving activities begin. Depending on the problem, a flow chart might be the first tool used by the team, particularly if the team disagrees about the flow of product or materials through the manufacturing or business processes. After the process is defined, it can also be applied in steps 1, 2, 3, and 4 of the Seven-Step Approach.

Who? The team leader, team, and facilitator. People outside the team or technical specialists may also be included to clarify information on the chart.

PROS AND CONS. Flow charts are easy to use.

Because they are pictorial, they are ideal for group work or for communicating a system's flow to others.

It takes patience to describe all the steps in a process accurately and list them on a chart. The result, however, serves as a benchmark for all other related studies. Flow charts also may be used for more than one problem-solving session.

Telephone Service Order Procedure

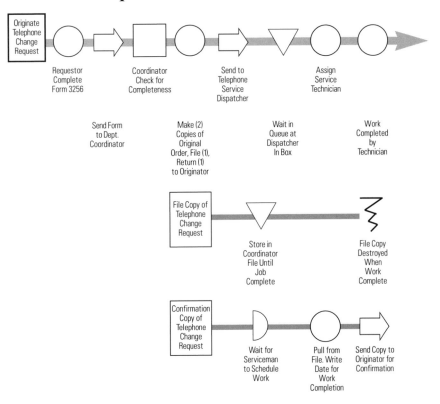

Figure 12.4. Flow Chart with ASME Symbols

SYSTEM FLOW CHART
Process Improvement

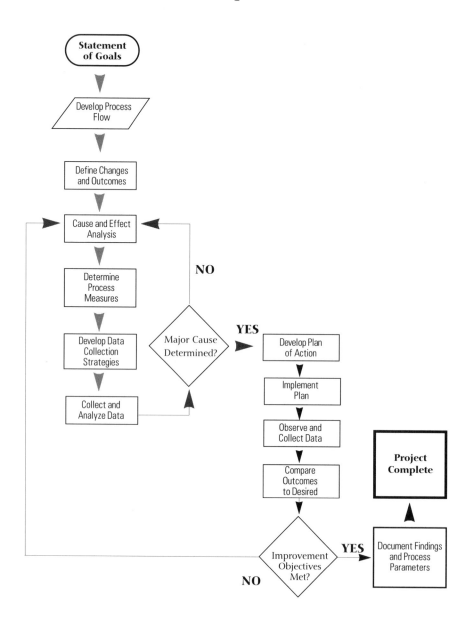

Figure 12.5   Flow Chart with Systems Symbols

Because flow charts are popular problem-solving tools, several types of symbol sets have also evolved. Occasionally, there may be confusion about the meaning of specific symbols. Generally, the team should start with and use one given set.

Hints. The flow chart is usually drawn horizontally, from left to right, because it may become necessary to extend the chart. Flow charting of reasonably complex processes literally may circle a good-sized room.

When using the flow charting technique, the team must define the boundaries of the study exactly–from "where" to "where" in the process with specific starting and ending points.

At the beginning of the exercise, the team must also decide what exactly is to be charted–person, material, product, or procedure. This must be constant. For example, if a single product is being charted, it cannot become a 144-count package shipping pallet later in the process. In each case, the chart should follow a consistent product and count.

Flow charts help teams understand exactly how things are being done. This can then determine how to improve that process. Because of this, the procedure may be applied to any phase of any activity anywhere in the entire organization. Any material, person, or thing that moves through a number of steps in a productive process may be charted.

Once a major change is made to a process, the chart should be updated.

Run Charts

What? Run charts, sometimes called trend charts, display measurements or information collected over specific time intervals: for example, a day, a week, or a month. It is actually a running tally or score of events.

How? Run charts are easily constructed and used. Points are plotted on a graph in the order they become available. Generally, the measurement being taken is plotted on the vertical axis in an appropriate scale, and time is plotted on the horizontal. Time may be an hour, day, week, or anything appropriate. The data being recorded may be a real measurement or quantity, or it may be a simple attribute (yes or no, pass or fail). Figure 12.6 shows a simple run chart.

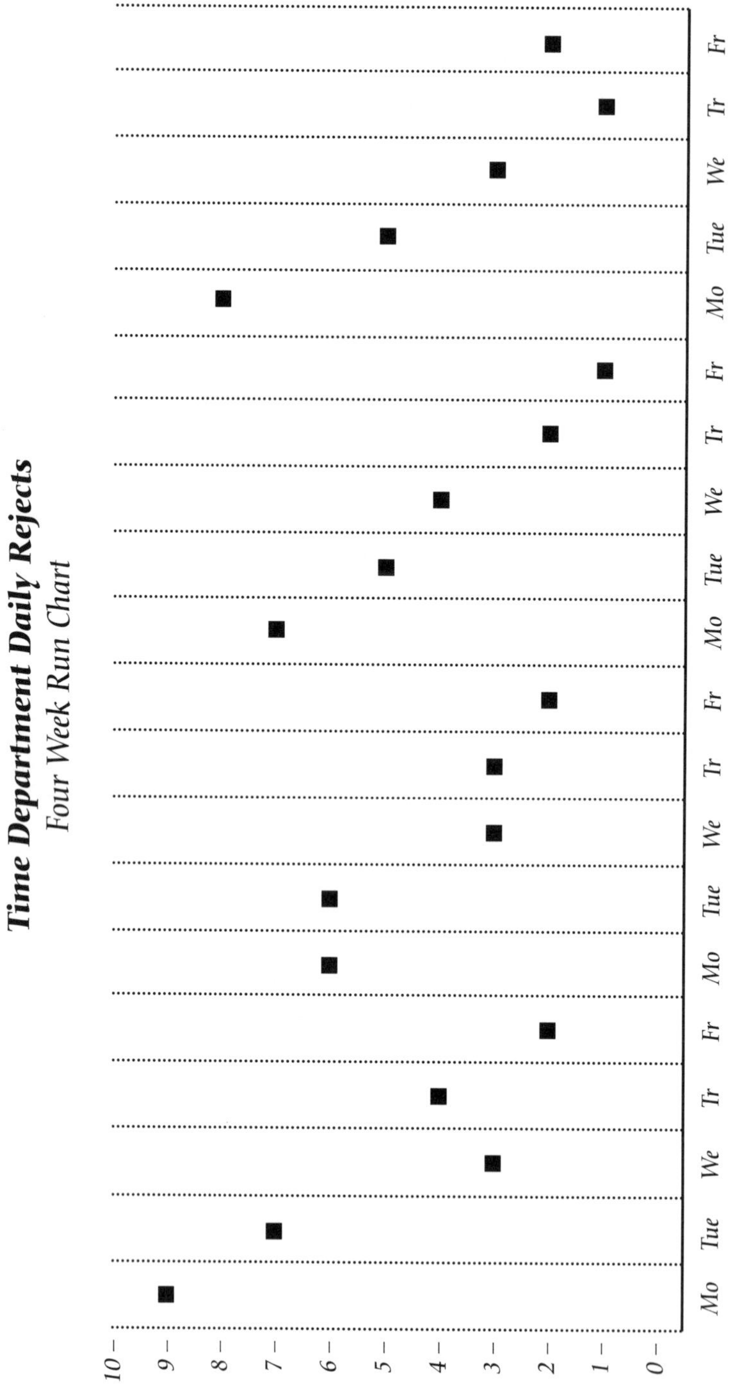

Figure 12.6. Run Chart

Why? To assist a team in gathering basic information about the day-to-day performance of equipment, manufacturing processes, or to gather data about a characteristic of any product or service.

When? A run chart is used when a simple record of events over a short period is necessary. Run charts may be used to plot machine yield, downtime, maintenance, scrap, or other factors influencing a process. The principal purpose of the chart is to spot trends. These are noticeable when the data shifts direction from the normal or average.

Run charts also help determine whether there are critical times during which problems of various types occur. The team can construct a run chart with quantity shown on the vertical axis and time along the horizontal axis. They then investigate the relationship, if any, between time of day and occurrence of problems. For example, a plot of defects by hour or day might show that problems consistently appear when materials from a certain supplier are used. Or, it may be found that a specific machine comes on line at the same time that certain problems appear. This suggests that the cause might lie with that machine.

In the Seven-Step Approach, run charts are most commonly used in steps 2 and 7.

Who? The team leader, team, and facilitator. Others outside the team may gather data or provide information.

PROS AND CONS. When a run chart is used, there can be a tendency to see every data variation as being important, or as being caused by a controllable problem. The run chart should be used only to focus attention on demonstrated process changes signified by long-term changes in trend. When any system is monitored, normal process variation will account for data fluctuation. If data follows an unusual trend, then it is reasonable to conclude that some outside factor has influenced the normal process

Hints. Data points should be plotted in the order they are collected (by day, hour, shifts, etc.). Connect the points with a line to show trends. Each data point indicates one measurement or characteristic, unless averages or some other indicators are being plotted. The vertical axis is always the measurement, and the horizontal is always time or a time period.

One method of determining a trend (positive or negative) is to view the data plotted and note how many consecutive times data falls above or below the average. In statistics, there is a theory of "runs" that is a good rule-of-thumb for determining whether data has become abnormal.

In normal operations, one would expect an equal number of data points above and below the average for a process. When the process is not stable, several consecutive points will fall outside the average in one direction. If nine or more consecutive points "run" on the high or low side of average, the natural variability of the process has changed. An investigation should be made. An alternative pattern is the run of sixes, where six or more consecutive points increase or decrease, with no reversals (each point has a value equal to or greater than the point before).

Sampling

What? In general, sampling is a process of collecting and analyzing a few bits of information (data) to obtain information about a large amount of data or an existing condition. In most instances, it is either impractical or impossible to study an entire population. A sample, by definition, is a certain number of objects or observations taken from a whole, or population, and used to obtain information about the whole. In statistics the term population means the total number of all conceivable objects of a given type under consideration. A population may be a large or small group of factory or office personnel, machines or equipment, piece parts or assemblies, or a combination of several.

Work sampling is used to analyze people's activities. Randomly taken observations determine the ratio of certain activities and elements to the total number of overall process observations. This ratio, or percentage, can accurately measure the activity's time as compared to the whole. The sample numbers are adjusted for the accuracy the answer requires. The greater the number of observations, the greater the final ratio's accuracy.

How? Sampling is based on the laws of probability. Sampling works because a small number of random occurrences usually follow the same distribution pattern of a larger number. For example, when a coin is tossed, the result is one of two possibilities: heads or tails. In 100 tosses, the laws of probability say that there will be exactly 50 heads and 50 tails. That is the ratio of the average possibilities, although each 100 tosses may not be exactly 50/50. As the coin is tossed more and more, the sample increases, and the distribution (or ratio) of heads and tails approaches 50/50, and the chance of error decreases with respect to the total accumulated sample.

A sampling study may be designed and implemented quickly. First, an observer determines the object(s) to be sampled. If that is a person or group, the team should determine what tentative activities will be observed (for example, machine operation, set-up, maintenance, cleanup, personal time, and so on). Within each of these elements, the study may also measure sub-items, such as gauging or material handling within the work cycle, or cause of idle downtime, such as tool changing, paperwork, supervisory instruction, and so on. Figure 12.7 shows sampling data for the status of

Machine Sampling Study Form

Work Element	Sample Observations	Total Observations	Percent
Machine Run	─╫╫╫ ╫╫╫ ╫╫╫ ╫╫╫ ╫╫╫ ╫╫╫ ╫╫╫ ╫╫╫ ╫╫╫ ╫╫╫ ╫╫╫ ╫╫╫ ╫╫╫ ╫╫╫ ╫╫╫ ╫╫╫ ╫╫╫ ╫╫╫ //	87	64.45
Down-Machine Setup	╫╫╫ //	7	5.19
Down-Machine Repair	╫╫╫	5	3.7
Down-Operator Absent/ Unknown Reason	///	3	2.22
Down-Operator Wait for Assistance	////	4	2.96
Down-Operator on Personal Time	╫╫╫ ///	8	5.93
Down-Material Problem	/	1	0.74
Down-Tool Change	//	2	1.48
Down-Tool Grinding	///	3	2.22
Down-Operator at Tool Crib	//	2	1.48
Down-First Piece Quality Check	///	3	2.22
Down-Material Handling	///	3	2.22
Down-Shift End Cleanup	////	4	2.96
Down-Clerical	/	1	0.74
Down-Receive Instruction	/	1	0.74
Down-Engineering	/	1	0.74
Total Samples		135	100.00

Percent Down TIme = **35.55**

Figure 12.7. Machine Sampling Study and Summary

115

machines, with relative run/down percentages and reasons for downtime.

If inanimate objects or machines are to be observed, there must be a tentative list of all conditions that might occur. In the case of a machine, the basic categories could be "run," "down," or "not scheduled." If downtime, the separate and distinct causes, such as tool changing, set-up, or lubrication might be considered. If manufactured parts or assemblies are to be sampled, the team must prepare a list of measurements, measurement ranges, or attributes to be noted in each sample.

After selecting the object of study, the team must then make only a few additional preparations. These include designing a form for recording data, deciding how often to observe the selection, (how many times per lot, batch, day, hour, or shift), and determining the random times or schedule for taking samples.

To indicate how the study is progressing, samples can be taken and summarized on a "running" basis. When an adequate number of samples has been taken, the study may be concluded.

Why? Sampling may be used to gather information about a work situation, process, or occurrence. When compared to observing and testing an entire event full time, sampling provides incomplete information. However, it may be used reliably within certain limits.

When? A sampling study is less complex than its alternatives, such as continually observing an event, or testing and checking all parts, pieces, machines, or processes. It may be used throughout the problem-solving process, but is rarely used to develop alternative solutions.

Who? The team leader, team, and facilitator. Others outside the team may gather data or provide information. An outside facilitator or consultant should assist the team in structuring a study.

PROS AND CONS. Teams typically do not have a great deal of time to study work situations, processes, or occurrences. Yet, information about such topics is necessary if a team is to draw any conclusions about them. Sampling may be used when a team needs information about a complex situation, system, or process quickly in order to define a problem.

In general, sampling has these advantages and characteristics:
- the principles and practice of sampling are easily understood;
- the technique may be applied to any object, animate or inanimate;
- sampling may be used to manage one's own time–

116

this is known as self-sampling;
- • resulting information is of known statistical accuracy;
- • distraction to the area or persons under study is minimized;
- • the sampling technique provides virtually any level of detail, depending on the study's design and how familiar the observer is with the object(s) being studied;
- • the technique can be applied simultaneously to large groups of objects; and
- • sampling requires a small investment in time.

Random observation times are necessary for maintaining statistical purity. They remove any partiality or prejudice an observer might introduce. Assuring randomness may be a problem for some groups or individuals, since samples must be taken during the entire time of an activity. In some instances, this may require "around-the-clock" commitments.

For their samples to yield accurate results, teams must assure a proper number of samples. An outside consultant or facilitator should be engaged to help the team set study parameters until it becomes comfortable with the technique.

Hints. Someone must assist in structuring the study and gathering data. Each member should take a turn at gathering data. The study time should initially be kept short so that results are produced as quickly as possible. The team then can move on, analyzing the information and formulating action plans. If samples are taken from individuals or groups, the team should involve those people in the study, let them know the objectives, outline the sampling plan and its time parameters. In no case should critical observations or notes be made about any individual's work habits, and all samples should be taken in an open, forthright manner.

Some work groups, individuals, and even managers and executives may have difficulty accepting the results of sampling studies. Many are not familiar with the technique, nor are they confident about its results. For this reason, early studies may find greater acceptance if they are limited to simple physical attributes, such as dimensions, color, or weight. In machine studies, a simple tally sheet with "run" and "down" categories, including a short list of reasons for downtime, may be useful. As the team becomes more proficient, much more comprehensive studies may be in order.

Check Sheets

What? Check sheets use essentially the same technique as sampling, except that a "100-percent sample" is taken. A particular activity or product is observed full-time during a prescribed period, and all passing or observed parts, characteristics, or actions are recorded on a form. The process is much simpler than sampling, because there are no random times to establish, and no statistical measures of accuracy to apply. Although the data gathering might still be termed a sample (since observation is made only over a selected interval), the data gathered absolutely reflects the conditions observed. There is no margin for error or questioning of the facts for that period.

How? Check sheets may be designed and used quickly. After determining the object(s) to be observed, the team lists all possible conditions. These may include measurements, simple attributes such as color and weight, or other product characteristics.

If a person or group is being observed, the team should determine what activities may take place. These may include machine operation, set-up, maintenance, cleanup, personal time, and so on. When observing machines, a team should try to list all conditions that might occur, such as maintenance, set-up, tool changing, and other machine-related activities. If parts or assemblies are being observed, the team must prepare a list of measurements, measurement ranges, or attributes.

After basic parameters of the study are determined, the team should design a form for recording tally marks. When enough tallies have been made to substantiate conclusions about the situation, the study may be concluded. Figure 12.8 shows a sample check sheet that assesses the average volume of process defects originating in a number of manufacturing departments.

Why? Check sheets are used to gather information about a work situation, process, or occurrence. Simply put, check sheets answer the questions about how often certain events in a process or business operation are happening. The check sheet is a simple methodology for developing information about a perceived problem, so that a course of action may be determined. Check sheets can determine the magnitude of a suspected problem, such as the percentage of certain defects in a department.

When? Check sheets may be used during the same phases of problem-solving as sampling. They are probably the most gathering data and information about a problem quickly.

Who? The team leader, team, and facilitator. Others outside the team may gather data or provide information. An outside facilitator or consultant can assist the team with developing a data format and recording initial information.

PROS AND CONS. Check sheets are less complex than other alternatives. In general, their advantages include:
- they are easy to use;
- they may be applied to any object, animate or inanimate;
- the information gathered is factual–it represents total occurrences over an established time period, rather than a sample computation;
- they can provide great detail, depending on the study design and how familiar the observer is with the object(s) under study.

Check sheets allow the team to accumulate information rapidly and convincingly.

Defects Reported by Production Week

Metal Fabrication	/////	/	///	///// /	////// ///	////	
Machining	//	/////	///	//	//// //// /	/	///
Metal Finishing	/	////// //	/	//			
Plating Shop	/		///		/	//	
Welding		//	/		///	/	//
Paint Shop	///	/	/		/		
Deburring	/	/	/		///	/	
Pack & Ship	//		/	/		/	
All Other Areas		//		//	/	/	/

Figure 12.8 Check Sheet for Recording Defects by Department

Depending on the problem, data gathered for an hour, a shift, or a day may satisfy the team's need. If more information is needed, the study can be restarted at any time, provided significant changes have not been made to the process.

Using a check sheet means stationing one or more observers at the process or procedure site over a continuous period. For example, someone might have to observe a machine over many days on several shifts to determine how frequently particular part defects or machine anomalies occur. Depending on the problem, sampling might be a less costly alternative, particularly for a team whose members have other pressing demands in the workplace.

Hints. The team must be prudent when defining the problem or issue it hopes the data it is gathering will address. Initial assistance in developing the check sheet activities to be tallied and the procedure for gathering data should be considered. Team members should take turns gathering data; this will assure cross-training and having more than one opinion of the activities. The study should initially be kept short. Producing results as quickly as possible will allow the team to move on.

All individuals or groups involved in the study should be informed of the data-gathering event, and permissions must be given where appropriate. No critical observations or notes should be permitted.

Scatter Diagrams

What? Scatter diagrams test whether there is a "cause and effect" relationship between any two factors. The factors may be such things as weight, strength, speed, distance, time, or almost any combination thereof that might be interdependent.

Scatter diagrams show how one variable relates to another. Sometimes these variables are called the "independent" variable and the "dependent" variable. They might also be called the "cause" and the "effect."

A scatter diagram is set up so that the horizontal axis represents measurements taken for one variable, and the vertical axis represents those for the second. Measurements are then plotted, with a data point placed at the intersection of the two values.

Several conclusions can be drawn from a scatter diagram. If the data points show a clear "pattern," this is called correlation. If there is an obvious correlation, it will be positive or negative. Further, it can be strongly positive or negative, or represent only a "possible" relationship. Finally, it can show no correlation, which means that there is no cause-and-effect relationship between the two factors selected.

On a graph, "positive" is up and to the right. This means that as one factor increases in value, so does the other. A "negative" relationship is one in which the X-axis variable gets smaller as the Y-axis variable is increased. No correlation exists when the data points appear to have no visible trend. Figure 12.9 shows a sample grouping of data from which conclusions about direction and correlation may be drawn. One obvious conclusion is that the taller men are, the more they weigh.

How? To construct a scatter diagram, collect several sets of data; a good sample in most situations is enough data to plot 30 to 50 points; more data (up to 100 points) is even better. Each point will be plotted from the horizontal and vertical axes of the chart, so each data set needs two values. Each point is based on what is called a "paired sample."

The diagram is drawn with the "cause" variable on the horizontal and the "effect" variable on the vertical. The scales on both axes should increase in value in the "up" direction or to the right. If values repeat after initial points are plotted, the repeating values should be circled as often as appropriate.

When all values are plotted, the team should search for a correlation and its direction. Is it positive or negative? If there is a clear correlation in either direction, a math formula can be used to predict the outcome using any value for the "cause" variable.

Why? To help a team determine the extent of a relationship between two factors in the system or work process.

When? Scatter diagrams may be used to define the true causes of a particular problem, or to test a theory about why a specific event might happen.

They are most commonly applied to steps 2 and 7 of the Seven-Step Approach.

Who? The team leader, team, and facilitator. People outside the team may contribute information or data for constructing the diagram. A consultant or other trained advisor may assist with statistical calculations. The technique can also be used by individuals alone.

PROS AND CONS. Scatter diagrams are easily drawn and used, but they can be confusing if the initial data does not correlate or if unrelated variables are inadvertently sampled. The technique does not yield a "yes or no" answer, but

121

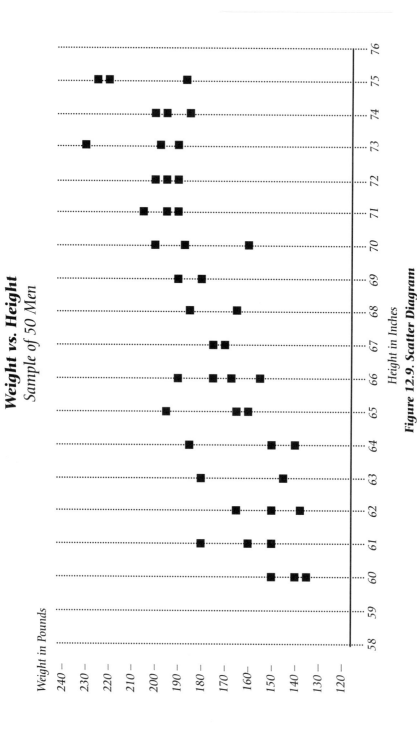

Weight vs. Height
Sample of 50 Men

Height in Inches

Figure 12.9. Scatter Diagram

122

must be studied before a conclusion can be reached. A particular problem may also have many causes; this would not appear in the relationship shown on a single scatter diagram.

Hints. Occasionally, scatter diagrams may show a definite correlation, but be limited by unknown factors in the process. For example, a trend may be quite obvious up to a certain variable value, and then "flatten out," or show no additional effect or correlation beyond that point. In effect, this puts a "kink" in the trend, and suggests that the relationship may only be good over a certain part of the process.

Histograms

What? A histogram is a special chart. It might also be considered a special form of the Pareto analysis. On this chart a number of separate, measured values for a particular product or process is represented by the length of a bar. Each category is labeled and the bars are placed next to one another, horizontally or vertically. This shows which categories account for most measured values, as well as the comparative size of each.

When the chart is built, the team will have a picture of the item in question's distribution. Most business or manufacturing processes, by their nature, have certain parameters that vary over time; each event does not repeat itself exactly from cycle to cycle. The histogram illustrates variability so that the process's stability can be judged.

How? Constructing a histogram is basically a simple process, but it is complicated somewhat by the fact that sizes for each collection class or cell must be decided. A class or cell is determined by its end points, high and low. For example, one bar on a histogram may be the number of measurements falling from 1.00 inch to 1.50 inches for a particular product. Every unit with a measured value in this range would therefore lengthen this bar on the chart. A value of 1.51 inches or higher would be posted to the next higher cell, and a value of 0.99 inch or below to the next lower cell.

However, it is still easy to prepare. First, the X- and Y-axes are labeled with the appropriate names and values. A number of data points are then gathered. Again, the larger the number of data points, the better and more conclusive the result on the histogram.

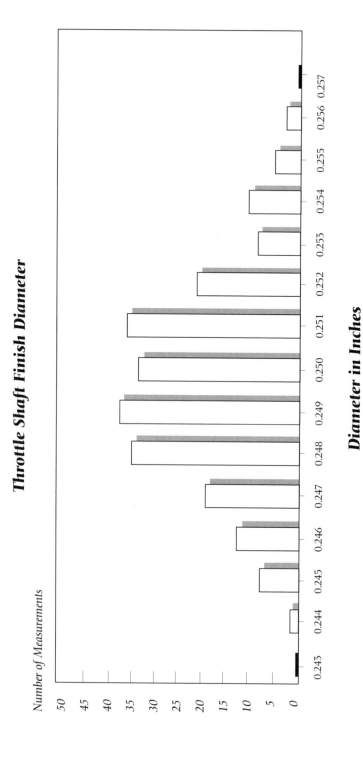

Figure 12.10. Histogram

Using information the team facilitator or another consultant has provided, the range (highest value to lowest value) of the data set is determined. This and the number of data points will statistically determine the number of classes (called also cells) into which the information will be entered. The process for determining the number of classes will also determine class width and set top and bottom points of each cell.

Once class widths are determined, the chart can be constructed. Either a mark is tallied or it is used to indicate how far the bar should extend. If desired, a separate tally sheet can be used before graphing. A sample histogram is shown in figure 12.10.

Why? To assist a team in determining whether variations in a process are normal and whether the process is under control. A normal distribution is (roughly shaped) like a bell. Histograms illustrate the distribution of actual outputs or results from a process.

When? A histogram is used when the team needs to focus on a process's variability to determine whether its normal output meets product specifications. Processes may also vary outside specifications and "lean" to the high or low side of specification; the histogram is a valuable tool for mapping this skewing of the process.

Histograms are most commonly used during steps 1, 2, and 7 of the Seven-Step Approach.

Who? The team leader, team, and facilitator. Data or information may be supplied by others outside the team. The technique can also be used by individuals alone.

PROS AND CONS. The histogram provides a "snapshot" view of variability. A quick glance at the chart can show an approximate average of all data, the range of occurrences, and whether the process is stable (a bell-shaped curve) or skewed in either direction. It can also indicate what portion of products are within, outside, or marginally close to specifications, high or low.

The team should note, however, that not all distributions follow a so-called normal curve. Some processes are completely under control even when they are skewed right or left, simply because that is the manufacturing plan. For example, for a product that is sold based on weight, it may be desirable to maintain a thickness on the specification's high side, rather than the middle.

Sometimes histograms are confusing and difficult to explain. For example, some charts may have two peaks, rather than one (this is called a bimodal distribution). Some cells may be empty. Some data may fall completely out of specification in one direction and not in the other.

Selecting class sizes properly is paramount. The number of classes (and therefore the number of bars in the graph) will determine how visible the pattern will be.

Hints. Histograms show two factors: variability and skewness. The width and shape of the bar pattern indicate variability and bars "clumped" to one side or the other of the establishing range indicate skewness.

Identifying a problem in variability or skewness and developing a course of action to correct it is the principal goal. The course of action involves several other technical steps, including calculating the mean of all sample data, calculating the standard deviation, and judging the process variation within statistical limits. It may also be beneficial to take many more measurements over time to assure the histogram's accuracy.

The team should make sure the data collection and measurement methods are consistent and accurate, that the process is running in an average manner, and that the calculations to establish cell sizes on the chart are correct. The team should use outside resource people to assist in defining classes and cell size and judging results.

Control Charts

What? Control charts continuously display the results of statistical process control measures. Control charts indicate several things, including whether measures of a product or activity fit a normal pattern (the bell-shaped curve). If the pattern is normal, then the work process is said to be "in control" because any measured variability in the product is random. By definition, if variations are random, they are not caused by some unknown outside error factor. Because control charts are clean and concise visual displays, an out-of-control process is easily and quickly noticed. The production process can then be corrected and brought back into control.

There are several types of control charts, the most common being the X-bar and R charts. Others are called p and np charts, and c and u charts.

X-bar and R charts deal with the size of variables (for example, a measurement or thickness), are used to track proportions (percentages) of attributes. Attributes are characteristics that are counted rather than measured with an instrument. Most of this discussion is concerned with X-bar and R charts.

How? A control chart may be seen as a run chart with statistically determined upper and lower limits drawn on either side of an average. The limits are calculated by gathering sample information about a process to determine the expected average value of a given measurement and then using specific statistical formulas.

In a normal or bell-shaped distribution, most of the measures are close to the overall mean or average; few things are ever exactly average. The typical or average difference of random measurements (as the product is produced over a period of time) taken from the overall mean is called the standard deviation. It is usually symbolized by the Greek letter sigma (s). The standard deviation tindicates how variable a measurement is.

If the process is under control, then the measurements form a normal distribution, with more than 99 percent falling somewhere between (+3) and (-3) standard deviations from the average. This means that a measurement so far above the average that it is more than three times the usual difference from the average is rare. Nor would one expect to obtain a measure so low as to be below the average by more than three times the usual difference from the average. Accordingly, (+3) standard deviations are known as the upper control limit (UCL), while (-3) standard deviations are called the lower control limit (LCL).

The UCL and LCL can be approximated if the average, the range, and the number of measures made are known. To set up a control chart, one must obtain sample measures and then determine the average and the range. Then the UCL and LCL can be calculated, based on variability estimates and assuming a normal distribution. Every control chart shows the UCL and LCL (in some cases, the LCL may be 0), so it is easy to determine whether the actual measures ever (or usually) exceed the UCL or go below the LCL. Figure 12.11 shows a conceptual model of a control chart. Note that in this simplified example, the process is "under control," with the data points well within the upper and lower limits.

After the chart and control limits are established, data is gathered periodically and consistently plotted on the chart. Usually, observing pattern and trend of data points will allow team members to determine whether the process is in control or not. Some point fluctuations within the limits represent the normal variability of the process; it is when a negative trend is noted or several data points exceed control limits that the process should be questioned.

Why? To assist in day-to-day determination of whether variations in a process are normal, and if the business or manufacturing process is currently under control.

When? Control charts are most commonly used in Step 7 of the Seven-Step Approach and beyond. Actually, control charts should be established and used consistently throughout the lifetime of a process. The charts offer a way to recognize problems before faulty material is sent to a customer. If proper control limits are established for each critical step in a manufacturing process, scrap and rework may be eliminated and a quality product passes on to the next user.

Who? The team leader, team, and facilitator. The technique can also be used by any work group, department, or individual able to gather daily process information.

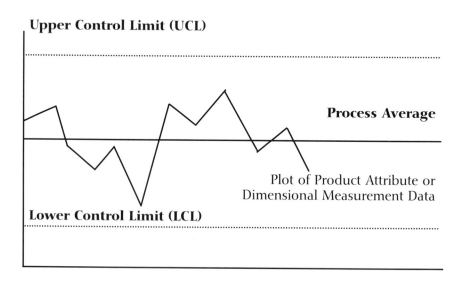

Figure 12.11. Model Control Chart

PROS AND CONS. Control charts are important and basic statistical process control tools.

They allow everyone associated with a manufacturing or business process or product to gain quality awareness. When control charts are posted conspicuously in a business or plant, everyone can see how well a process is performing. Further, the charts help to maintain a sense of urgency when problems arise. Any control that will be used to monitor a process in the long term should be displayed as close to the actual process as possible. The chart should be enlarged if necessary.

A common mistake is using these charts to "control everything." Charts should be used with caution, and generally only for those processes critical to producing a quality product. Too many charts and too much data make it difficult to understand the process's true nature and critical points.

Unfortunately, it takes training and expertise to construct control charts correctly. Also, there are many types of charts, each designed for a specific purpose and requiring special structure and limits calculations. For this reason, the team facilitator, consultant, or another experienced person should guide the team when control charts are to be used. Since there are numerous types of control charts that may be used to map both attribute-type information and dimensional data, the team facilitator or consultant should assist the team with control chart design   until the team members understand the charting principles.

Finally, control charts may not be the proper tool for solving all process-related problems. There are many other techniques that are simpler to use and understand.

Hints. When you use control charts, remember that a process "in control" doesn't necessarily mean the process is good. The data may be consistently poor without exceeding a control limit.

Even when measurements show that the process is in control, the average may still be off-target, too high or too low. Further, the amount of variation may be much greater than an "ideal" process needs. A control chart can help identify the reasons for those conditions and can be used to correct them.

Upper and lower control limits do not mean the drawing's or specification's limits. Based on the samples used to calculate limits for a "three sigma" distribution, the control limits may be either more or less than the product's normal specifications. It is therefore possible that a process could be "under control" and still be making scrap parts.

There are many statistical rules for interpreting control charts. These should be understood by the team when appropriate and necessary. Generally, "out-of-control" conditions may be caused by:

- accuracy of measurements taken for charting;
- differences in methods applied between shifts or operators;
- environmental factors, such as temperature and humidity;
- wear of critical tools or equipment;
- use of untrained personnel;
- changes in maintenance schedules;
- change of raw or consumable materials used in the process; and
- inconsistent data from multiple machines, operators, or shifts.

Teams should be aware of these conditions and address them accordingly.

Summary

THIS CHAPTER HAS NOT ADDRESSED ALL the problem-solving techniques a team might use in a given situation; there are many more available. Further, there are a significant number of proprietary approaches. However, if a team has mastered the techniques listed here, there will be little general use for other methods. Two exceptions would be other types of control charting techniques and perhaps the application of Taguchi methods for design of experiments. The mechanics of these and other approaches are readily found from libraries, bookstores, or professional organizations.

CHAPTER 13

RECOGNITION

"Things may come to those who wait,
but only the things left by those who hustle."

– ABRAHAM LINCOLN

COMPANY CULTURE CAN BE ALTERED significantly and influenced substantially by the judicious use of employee incentives. More than simple certificates, cash, merchandise, or "pats on the back," the process of recognition is becoming a social science and a field of its own.

The time-worn process of employee "giveaways," such as cash, trips, gifts, and accolades for top-performing people, is now secondary to praising genuinely all firm members for work well done. Giveaway programs are simply not appropriate for the work environments that emphasize employee empowerment, teamwork, and ownership.

What is Recognition?

RECOGNITION IS A FORM OF EMPLOYEE motivation. A firm recognizes, praises, and thanks employees and groups that have made positive contributions to the enterprise's success. In an ideal world, every employee enjoys the challenges of his or her job, and motivation results from pride in workmanship or in work well done. In the practical real world, however, managers must be sensitive to people's changing needs and wants, and be aware that a recognition system is a dynamic and necessary part of business planning.

Some executives and managers view recognition systems as motivational stimulants that increase organizational productivity. Presumably, those not working to capacity will improve if they are given some sort of incentive, usually cash, above and beyond their normal stipend. This approach assumes, of course, that the incentive provides or increases motivation. Some authors argue that motivational "gifts" defeat such intrinsic motivators as pride of workmanship that might currently be driving employee behavior. Further, the values set as acceptable by a firm's managers may not be the same as those expected or set by its employees. Management cannot proclaim that its major focus is customer satisfaction if it fails to reward those who have been praised by customers. It also makes little sense to award prizes for recruiting new customers if old customers are dropping away because they are being neglected or receiving poor service.

Recognition systems offer incentives for improved work quality or greater productivity. Of greater importance, however, is the recognition system a firm adopts. This makes a statement about the principles important to the company. The method and extent of recognition in a company provide insight into the firm's management values.

Objectives and Values

AT THE BEGINNING, THE TQ VISIONARY must establish objectives–those principles that will be observed when a recognition and reward program is being administered. For example, will all personnel in the firm be able to participate? Will there be recognition for individuals only, teams only, or both? In what combination and on what occasions? Will customers and vendors be allowed to participate when appropriate? What are the financial and time resources that may limit award distributions? What current recognition programs exist? Are there conflicts in charters between them and the TQ initiative? Can existing programs be curtailed if they are no longer useful?

How recognition and award programs for significant accomplishments are administered reflects the attitudes and values of those who have initiated TQ. TQ cannot be effected without considering one of the "perils" of TQM success: how to reward contributor successes and continue to maintain quality and productivity motivation.

Key Attitudes

THERE ARE SEVERAL KEY BEHAVIORS and attitudes that a visionary manager or executive must establish by developing employee award and recognition systems guidelines. These apply equally well to any number of management initiatives, within and outside a TQ context.

Sincerity. Management must sincerely and honestly wish to recognize individual and group efforts toward ensuring the success of the enterprise. Using recognition to reward or payoff routine or non–specific performance is not a sound foundation for the system. Sincere recognition means saying "thank you!" for a job done well in what may have been difficult circumstances.

Fairness. Managers cannot play favorites, nor can they hold one employee team or work group in higher financial regard than others. Recognition and award guidelines demand equal treatment for equal accomplishments. By definition, this indicates that equal and unbiased consideration must be given to both hourly and salaried business groups. Many times, executives deliberately exclude certain employee groups from specific awards, since they are perceived to "make enough already." This is patently unfair and eventually leads to employee turnover or lessened motivation. Every employee appreciates recognition when and if the occasion warrants.

Appropriateness. The TQ steering committee must provide ground-rules that guide awards and recognition in the TQM initiative. Clear and definitive boundaries must be set, and they cannot be applied only to monetary awards given for quality and productivity improvements. Awards may be commendations, lunches, dinners, trips, merchandise certificates, or a visit from the CEO. Whatever the award, however, the level must be appropriate to the improvement made. Further, the steering group should also arrange to award improvements in safety, housekeeping, vendor and customer relations, and other intangible areas. Accomplishments that should not be awarded are those which are considered part of the work assignment, such as "perfect attendance."

Consistency. Guidelines developed by the TQ steering committee must be applied throughout the organization consistently. If award systems are not policed and monitored, they may become negative motivators. Many so-called employee suggestion systems in the United States are a good example. Employees simply refuse to participate in the programs. This in turn inflicts grievous penalties on American competitiveness.

Timeliness. Recognition and any subsequent award must be timely. The team, employee, or work group is excited about its accomplishment now, not weeks or months into the future. Do not allow significant actions to go unrewarded (or unacknowledged) beyond the current team reporting period, whether it is a week, two weeks, or a month. Use team accomplishments and rewards to "pump up the troops," encouraging competition among and between organizations. Make each and every team accomplishment, particularly those involving external customers, a great and unforgettable occasion. Solicit teams for ideas on how to provide the recognition and how to keep it timely.

Importance. Recognition in any form is important to the recipients. Managers, supervisors, executives, and peers must be given the opportunity to share successes with time and occasion for joining in the emotions and feelings of the moment. Every award winner should feel that he or she is the focus of all activity for the moment. Every contribution made by any employee deserves attention; if that attention is sincere and consistent, most employees will accelerate their efforts toward the next goal.

Characteristics of Recognition Systems

POSITIVE AND SUCCESSFUL EMPLOYEE recognition systems are defined by specific characteristics. They differ from "giveaway" programs, suggestion systems, or "carrot and stick" motivational programs.

Recognition is not compensation. First and foremost, recognition programs must not be used as substitutes for normal and fair compensation. Compensation is based on employee status, job tenure, training, skill levels, and a host of other factors not related to motivation levels. Further, compensation policy is not personalized, is firmly established by long-term company policy and procedures, and generally is not flexible. Recognition, in comparison, is flexible, personalized, and based on immediate accomplishments.

There are no "winners" and "losers." The recognition system must be structured so that persons or groups are not ranked. Awards made time and again to certain groups will create a stigma that identifies particular groups or individuals as "losers." Those being recognized will always feel good, and those that are not will feel bad. If favorite department members or special support personnel are recognized repeatedly over time, the positive reinforcement and motivational values will be lost. Recognition has to be valid, genuine, and a meaningful experience for the giver and the recipient. Also, those who are always recognized may even become complacent, believing that they should be rewarded because they always are and not because of special accomplishment. Eventually, the effect will be demotivating and demoralizing. This will also cause the formation of social classes or "castes" among the workforce.

Studies have confirmed that those consistently on the short end of rewards will eventually cease to perform effectively, defeating many of the recognition program's original intents.

Not all successes are measured. Many times, there should be recognition for above-average efforts expended in tackling intangible or not easily quantified issues. Safety is an important intangible; so are customer goodwill and satisfaction. To accommodate intangibles, recognition may be made based on efforts, not just quantified results obtained. It is difficult to measure employee morale, long-term process improvement, or technological change, but these changes are essential to a company's good health.

Recognition is not manipulation. Managers and executives must avoid using recognition to promote a conditioned behavior. Recognition systems must not be used to coerce or otherwise encourage changes in behavior patterns. Nor should they be used to re-order a priority of tasks, or to accomplish quotas. For example, in manufacturing there is the continuing conflict among three principal factors: cost, schedule, and quality. A recognition system cannot reward accomplishments in quality to the exclusion of productivity improvements or scheduling accomplishment. Further, if quality is emphasized over productivity, then the company may be sending the wrong, or a mixed, message to employees.

In an improperly managed recognition program, awards may be given that are totally inconsistent with stated management values. A review of recognition practices and programs will show whether the rewards given are consistent with the mission and values of the company, and whether the proper "messages" are being sent to the workforce. An employee cannot receive a reward for improving quality and be reprimanded at the same time for a production quota shortfall. If customer satisfaction and goodwill are important, then awards cannot be given only for increased sales dollars. If on-time shipments are important, then awards should be given for schedule accomplishments plus quality level. Management must mean what it says, and demonstrate it by action.

Recognition is not based on luck or "fate." Reward must be related to work accomplishment, to the absolute exclusion of any doubt. Awards must be based on fact–documented actions that demonstrate that an award is appropriate and consistent with the accomplishment itself. If employees come to believe that rewards are based on "luck of the draw," they will eventually cease all but the most structured activities and become demoralized and static.

Cynics abound in an organization that does not consistently and equitably compensate its employees, both in recognition programs and in wage structure. As cynicism develops, employees and management are cast into an "us versus them" scenario, and workers accept the view that all management initiatives are new attempts to dehumanize and exploit.

Employees contribute to the recognition strategy. Ownership of and total commitment to a recognition policy and procedures are possible when employee input has been solicited during policy decisions. Employees must be given the knowledge and tools for making rational decisions about the quantity, quality, and logistics of recognition. Management should be involved only when it becomes necessary to establish ground rules, boundaries, and priorities. The expectations and perceptions of employees should be surveyed before a system or plan alteration is implemented. This is a good time to use an outside consultant, who will provide the objectivity normally not found in an organization. All parties involved must make sure that the accomplishments management wants to recognize are visible to employees, and vice-versa. The program must establish a values hierarchy.

It is good practice to select employee committees to review recognition criteria and policies. These should represent a fair cross-section of the organization's population as well as the company's unions or skilled trades groups. This approach helps the planning process and negates perceptions that management is using recognition to manipulate.

Recognition is a personal experience. Management should attempt to give recognition to individual efforts when it is possible. If a "head-and-shoulders above" employee cannot be identified, commendation should be made to several individuals that comprise a given team. Individuals should be recognized by name and, if possible, at random.

In any case, recognition should never imply a caste system, wherein managers (superiors of more importance) reward employees (subordinates of less importance). Instead, all employees and teams should be given an equal opportunity to select how the reward should be presented, what it should be, and who should receive it.

Recognition is fun. Award ceremonies should be planned and scheduled as if they were an important business meeting. The meeting time and place should be at the award winner's convenience, for he or she is the "guest of honor." Once called to order, the occasion should be treated as a time to celebrate. Celebrity guests or speakers are certainly welcome, but the employee should take precedence if there are schedule conflicts. Finally, recognition cannot become mired in a bureaucratic process.

Recognition can be given both privately and publicly. Generally, public commendation is superior to private, simply because most people enjoy receiving kudos from a group. Also, public presentation can serve as a good communications medium for management. It allows current issues and goals to be emphasized.

Occasionally, there will be certain employees that are uncomfortable with public presentations. If this occurs, the presenting manager or organization should accede to the wishes of the recipient and revise the ceremony type and location.

Using employee peers to recommend and present certain levels or types of awards is a successful recognition approach. "Peer-to-peer" award has several distinct advantages over other approaches. Using employee peers removes much of the anti-company or anti-management cynicism that sometimes accompanies teambuilding and TQ. The peer approach also solidifies cooperative objectives, since success or failure rests with peers and coworkers, not managers. Potential roadblocks in the superior-to-subordinate relationship are overcome.

The peer award focuses and promotes quality and productivity efforts aimed at the "internal customer." In this case, this is another employee, team, or group who has found an individual's or group's performance to be exceptional. This use of intra-organizational kudos promotes continued cooperation and teamwork.

As with any recognition system, peer-to-peer award criteria must be well documented and applied with prudence.

Innovation in Recognition

FORMS OF RECOGNITION MAY RANGE from certificates to plaques to cash or merchandise awards. If cash awards are given, great care should be taken to assure that a pattern or trend is not developing. Ongoing awards of substantial cash sums or large merchandise certificates might cause problems with the system. When too much cash passes hands on a regular basis, employees tend to treat the awards as part of normal compensation similar to "regular overtime." When this happens, employees and their families come to expect award income. They lose the pride associated with special gifts given for unusual accomplishments. If such a system exists, and then is taken away or modified, management risks losing confidence and trust in TQ and teambuilding.

While routine large cash awards should be discouraged, there is no question that cash or near-cash is a motivator in the workplace. It therefore should be a staple form of recognition in any organization that has a formalized program for rewarding outstanding achievements. If cash or cash equivalents are to be used, the following recommendations should be considered.

Give away real money, not company checks. Nothing grabs attention faster than handing someone portraits of dead American presidents. Using checks compounds the bureaucratic nature of the system.

Pre-pay taxes for the employee. The award should be a net amount and should not be influenced by any further payroll deduction. Also, an award should not bring the individuals year-end tax liabilities.

In lieu of cash, award useful merchandise. Grocery or gasoline certificates that may be used widely are excellent awards.

Involve the spouse. If sports, theater, or dinner tickets are considered, award them in pairs so that the recipient and a guest may use them. For special occasions, send flowers or steaks.

When the occasion demands, celebrate victories as a team. Book a bus for a day trip, or a hay wagon for a weekend cookout and hayride. Arrange special group lunches or dinners in the plant or off-site.

Make a gift to charity in the name of a recipient. This is extraordinarily powerful if an individual is involved in a special charity or cause. Similarly, making a suitable gift to a favorite educational institution (many companies match awards at a corporate level, thereby doubling the original amount) is often quite effective. The individual should be given a formal notice and receipt, and the gift should be publicly disclosed.

Involve customers and vendors. Celebrate accomplishments that have earned suppliers or clients specific benefits by collectively "toasting to continued successes and good relations."

Avoid trophies, plaques, and certificates. Unless inscribed with individual names, this type of award tends to lose significance with time. Often they end up being tossed aside and forgotten. If certificates are necessary, make sure they are in good frames that may be used for other purposes.

Award cash in unique and fun ways. Place bills in a picture-frame that can be used later for a family or child portrait. Present a $50 award as a padded pack of fifty new, crisp, one-dollar bills. Buy padding cement at a local printer, stack the bills on a piece of chipboard and coat one end of the stack with padding cement. When the stack is dry, bills can be torn off the stack like checks from a checkbook. When asked by the curious, the recipient can joke that money is cheaper when purchased from the government in "books."

Make good use of U. S. Savings Bonds. Consider awarding bonds in the name of an employee's child (note that the bond application must include either the child's or the parent's social security number).

Buy fast food gift certificates. For most people, these are useful and appreciated gifts.

Lessons Learned About Recognition

WHILE RECOGNITION PROGRAMS PROMOTE teambuilding and TQ initiatives, installing a successful and equitable program requires great thought and thorough planning from many interests. Caution and slow–but–steady progress are the orders of the day. A few lessons learned from business and industry are outlined below.

Outside assistance will probably be necessary, particularly for establishing and evaluating the program. This may be another role for the TQM and teambuilding consultant.

Each business location and employee/management organization is probably unique. It cannot be assumed that successful systems from one corporate location can be successful in another. Plan for substantial monitoring.

The recognition system must be based on the published visions, mission, values, and principles of the firm. Document and communicate guidelines clearly. In the event of ambiguity, the steering committee or executive management must make timely resolution.

Use common sense. There are finite and rational boundaries in any system of award and reward.

Recognition is special. It is not compensation.

The personal touch is important. Bureaucracies cannot grant meaningful recognition. People can.

All systems require review, modification, and revision as time passes and employees move on. Management must consciously plan to examine the recognition system for efficacy regularly.

CHAPTER 14

THE TIME LINE

"Success is never final."

– WINSTON CHURCHILL

A TIME-PHASED PLAN FOR INSTALLING a teambuilding and TQM initiative is discussed in this chapter. The plan is based on a three-year period–the nominal time necessary for bringing a TQ concept to fruition. This plan is not the definitive answer; it is simply a guide. The sequence of events, however, is rational and important to its overall success. The visionary executive should take care to follow each step; there are no real shortcuts. Also, depending on resources and other business priorities, some activities may lag behind or lead the proposed schedule.

Another factor in timing is the business's overall size and diversity. A small, compact firm with few employees may be organized and trained for TQM with less effort and logistics problems than a larger one. Further, a process-oriented industry, such as oil, mining, paper, or plastics may be easier to organize than a manufacturer and assembler of diverse consumer products. A very large operation, with many functions and departments all located at one site, may need outside consultants, trainers, or facilitators, or a "train-the-trainer" program phase.

For convenience, time periods are established as quarters, and actions are roughly in order within each period. "Year One, Quarter One," starts with the visionary's decision to commit to the initiative. The plan assumes that regular (weekly or biweekly) team and steering committee meetings will be held after the organizational and initial training sessions; on-going routine events are therefore not listed.

Year One, Quarter One

1. Commitment decision is made.
2. Develop "first-cut" plan for Year One.
3. Select associate or subordinate to act as "junior visionary" and assist in the overall strategy.
4. Procure, review, and complete applications for membership in select professional organizations (descriptions and addresses may be found in any public library). A partial list includes:
   - American Quality and Productivity Center;
   - American Society for Quality Control (ASQC);
   - American Society for Training and Development (ASTD);
   - Association for Quality and Participation;
   - Institute of Industrial Engineers (IIE);
   - Quality and Productivity Management Association;
   - Society for Human Resource Development (SHRD); and
   - Society of Manufacturing Engineers (SME).
5. Establish TQM and teambuilding libraries and resource files. Review and obtain current management texts on quality topics (continuing).
6. Review and obtain available audio-visual materials (continuing).
7. Solicit marketing materials from select consultants or firms.
8. Select steering committee (TEAM1) members.
9. Hold briefing meetings for steering committee.
10. Establish a plan for reviewing, critiquing, and selecting consulting resources.
11. Develop the fundamental vision of the organization that will be used to write the mission statement.

Year One, Quarter Two

1. Rank consulting resources and solicit on-site presentations, followed by formal proposals.
2. Contract a consultant.
3. Request a detailed plan for the first six months of proposed activities.
4. Present consulting plan to steering committee for design review/critique.
5. Develop a time-phased plan and appropriate milestones. Formulate the mission statement and guiding principles and values.
6. Develop a name, theme, and graphic model of interactions and organizational responsibilities.
7. Draft and publish a TQM operating procedure.
8. Develop a team structure and reporting hierarchy.
9. Select initial departments, team leaders, facilitators, and team members.

Year One, Quarter Three

1. Develop COQ benchmarks.
2. Design a survey instrument for assessing employee attitudes about quality and team topics.
3. Survey pilot group (steering committee and selected staff); recap and edit survey content as required.
4. Integrate survey results and perceptions into the TQ plan.
5. Present plan to management and staff.
6. Present plan to prospective team leaders and facilitators.
7. Present plan to union leadership (as applicable).
8. Steering committee prepares company-wide kickoff plans.

Year One, Quarter Four

1. Develop training syllabus for team leaders and facilitators.
2. Design and start publishing a monthly or bimonthly TQM employee newsletter; make assignments and arrangements for editing, production, and employee inputs.

3. Hold a TQM kickoff event.

4. Develop and gain approval for second year activities.

5. Develop plan to commemorate the first year anniversary.

Year Two, Quarter One

1. Celebrate the initiative's first-year anniversary.

2. Present teambuilding training to team leaders and facilitators.

3. Develop training syllabus for team members.

4. Survey remaining workforce; recap survey results, compare them with pilot group data, and publish results and conclusions.

5. Revise or modify goals as appropriate.

6. Assess results and feedback of team leader and facilitator training sessions in informal steering committee reviews.

Year Two, Quarter Two

1. Present teambuilding training to team members.

2. Present problem-solving technique training to team leaders and facilitators (basic tools).

3. Conduct initial team meetings. Select and train additional teams in teambuilding and basic problem-solving techniques.

4. Develop and present advanced problem-solving techniques to specific teams as appropriate.

5. Assign a steering committee coordinator to track and monitor the status of all projects listed on team action logs.

6. Assess results of each team meeting and project actions in informal steering committee reviews.

Year Two, Quarter Three

1. Organize new teams as initial teams mature and become more autonomous.

2. Continue problem-solving training for members of newly organized teams as required (basic tools).

3. Continue presentation of advanced problem-solving techniques to specific teams as appropriate.

4. Develop team-led presentations for lower and mid-management to emphasize experiences and successes and to

develop experience in presentation techniques.

5. Develop a plan to communicate goals and TQM philosophy to critical and high dollar-volume vendors and suppliers.

6. Request vendor and supplier responses and TQ plans.

Year Two, Quarter Four

1. Plan a major process review for executive management; solicit individual team leaders and members to prepare and deliver reports on projects, status, and successes.

2. Develop and gain approval for third year activities.

Year Three, Quarter One

1. Implement vendor and supplier TQM initiatives.

2. Develop "partnering" agreements if appropriate. Develop a comparison of current COQ indicators with pre-TQM benchmarks (indicators should be evaluated annually or biennially hereafter).

3. Train all remaining team leaders, teams, and facilitators.

4. Assist vendors and suppliers with development of their own training programs and procedures.

Year Three, Quarter Two

1. Survey all employees about their attitudes and perceptions, using the survey instrument designed in the first year.

2. Present survey results to steering committee, union leadership (if applicable), and remaining workforce.

3. Revise or modify plans as appropriate, based on issues raised by survey.

Year Three, Quarter Three

1. Initiate planning for phasing out external facilitation and consultant services.

2. Assure that all initiative-related policies and procedures are well-documented and in a central file.

3. Back up computer files and training materials.

Year Three, Quarter Four

1. Design an instrument or checklist for a continuing internal audit of the initiative's health and vitality.

2. Establish a plan for sustaining periodic external consultant reviews.

3. Consultant(s) perform outgoing audit and prepare and present a "state of the initiative" review to steering committee and executive management.

Summary

CHANGING A BUSINESS CULTURE is not a short-term proposition, and installing TQM is a daunting task.

Many teambuilding and TQM installations have failed because results have been expected too soon or a definite, calculated payback has been demanded too soon. CEOs, business managers, and major stockholders are notorious for expecting quick and short-term actions and techniques.

Building a self-sustaining TQ team takes years, not months, of work. The time frame cannot be compressed. The culture shock TQ administers to employees, supervisors, managers, and executives means taking time to soothe ruffled feathers, while cultivating the attitudes necessary for building trust and teamwork.

CHAPTER 15

AVOIDING FAILURE

"What the company wants is for us to work like the Japanese.
Everybody go out and do jumping jacks in the morning
and kiss each other when they go home at night.
You work as a team, rat on each other, and lose control of
your destiny. That's not going to work in this country."

– JOHN BRODIC, UNITED PAPERWORKERS, AS QUOTED IN BUSINESS WEEK

THERE ARE SEVERAL SIGNS THAT CLEARLY warn that a TQ initiative may be proceeding in the wrong direction or pursuing a developmental activity too quickly, too slowly, or out of logical sequence. This chapter describes symptoms that may indicate potential large-scale problems in system implementation, and includes cautionary comments for the visionary executive.

Strategic Problems

OF ALL POTENTIAL PROBLEMS AND ROADBLOCKS, those of a strategic nature are the most significant. They can derail an entire system and any initiatives in place at the time. Fortunately, many strategic issues are not insidious or intangible; curing the problems is generally a matter of simply doing the right thing or taking the right direction.

Don't give up too soon. Every TQM installation creates anxiety, frustration, irritation, and the burning desire to "get something done...now!" The natural tendency of most managers is to get through the process and to the result as soon as possible. The TQ implementation process is a multiyear project; after that, it's a lifetime commitment. The visionary executive, his or her staff, and the steering committee must attend to the many intricacies of mission, values, procedures, teambuilding, training, and communication. When all elements are done properly and in sequence, results will come.

Don't promise anything to anybody. TQ benefits are not based on paybacks or a specific financial performance within any finite time period. Changing a culture takes time and provides many intangible results. The implementation of a continuous improvement process cannot be measured or ratified in any form other than qualitatively assessing program milestones. Some of the greatest business benefits, those of creating and holding markets and developing customer satisfaction and allegiance, will not be assessed for years.

Choose teams carefully. Initial team leaders and their team members must be chosen for success. While it might seem democratic for every natural work group leader to lead a TQ team in an initiative's formative days, the visionary executive and steering committee must purposely discriminate. Choose the best and most insightful leaders first. It is not necessary to publicize the selection process (it should be done confidentially by the visionary executive and steering committee). The company's best leadership potential must be used first. As these employees mature as TQ team leaders, their success stories and expertise will spread to other, less talented peers. Success breeds more success.

Choose projects to assure success. Many would call this "cherry-picking," or harvesting the "low-hanging fruit." Whatever it is called, plan initial projects to ensure success. In the long run, teams will gain confidence rapidly and mature into elite problem-solving brigades. At the present, however, the company should not relegate "impossible" problems or tasks to the new teams. The newly formed team is not an elite unit with instant skills for performing where others have failed. Assigning tenuous tasks will create roadblocks that hinder commitment. Eventually, lack of progress will demotivate the team, perhaps irreparably.

Don't treat TQM as a tool to improve manufacturing quality or productivity. TQ awareness and the teambuilding process are culture-changing initiatives that must affect the entire organization. That should be made clear from the very beginning. The organization cannot be allowed to view TQM as a tool, new technique, program-of-the-day, or anything but an absolute change in strategic thinking.

The entire organization consists of customers. Every employee must understand that he or she is also a client that receives products and services, and that internal and external customers are entitled to superior value. Team goals and objectives should address each step in the value-adding process, from one end of the organization to the other. Any small improvement in quality or productivity will be magnified when the product or service is presented to the final customer.

Delegate, groom, and train. The visionary executive must continually prepare others to carry out TQ tasks in the event of absence or organizational change. One individual cannot cheerlead a TQ crusade for long. Other managers must be motivated and qualified enough to share responsibilities and rewards. "Assistant visionaries" should be selected early and groomed constantly.

Have fun. Any individual will contribute significantly in a work atmosphere that encourages fellowship, camaraderie, and celebration for and recognition of success. Everyone in the organization must be given an opportunity to enjoy work assignments and work associations. This is an essential corollary to the eighth of Dr. W. Edwards Deming's famous fourteen points–"drive out fear."

Training Ills

MANY POTENTIAL ILLS HAVE TO do with the training process, simply because training is so tightly woven into TQ planning.

Don't train too much too quickly. Many companies have committed serious TQM installation errors by buying into large, sometimes "off-the-shelf," training programs and dispensing varying degrees of quality training topics across the organization. Too often, groups of employees are sent to seminars for a day or two and expected to acquire fully all the skills needed to perpetuate the team for the next generation. It simply will not happen. Before any training investment is made, a needs assessment must be done. Functionally, this must be done for all employees and management levels. It is a major step in the TQM planning process. Employee teams, leaders, and facilitators cannot be "solutions in search of problems." Further, there is substantial data to indicate that newly acquired skills, particularly in technical topics, can dissipate quickly if they are not used routinely and frequently.

Unfortunately, many trainers and training consulting organizations fail to assess needs properly before beginning the training. They feel business may be lost if a particular program is postponed. Also, individuals and teams themselves often believe training is prerequisite to success, so it must be done right away. However, few are able to assess needs without having met as teams to define those problems that need solutions.

It is difficult to determine whether teams benefit from large doses of quick training. Many teams, lacking training, tend to "fix" their own problems without intervention, and will continue to do so as long as their resourcefulness is properly recognized. The best role to be served by team leaders and facilitators is to help teams understand their own strengths and limitations.

Training alone will not build teamwork. Training introduces tools and techniques that help employees and their teams harness their innate creativity and innovation. Team members must integrate this training with other skills if they want to interact properly with their peers and company management.

Training doesn't end when a group leaves the classroom. If training programs are presented logically, the newly discovered tools and techniques should be immediately applicable to the problems in the workplace. Also, learning must take place outside the classroom, as well as in it.

A significant milestone is reached when individual teams, having worked together on several projects, recognize specific shortfalls in their collective skills and request additional training. At this point, the team is close to being self-perpetuating and self-nurturing.

Train people in team groups, not individually. Team members cannot be trained as entities. Classes or seminars are not "career development" opportunities for individuals alone. When teams are trained as a group, they feel firsthand that the training requires participation and involvement in the teambuilding process. They can confirm what they have learned as a group, and discuss workplace application. Trainers can solicit classroom commitments from the team members to apply new knowledge to certain projects. Further, all members assume an implicit responsibility for paying back the company for its training investment.

Many organizations feel that their business can't afford to lose a work group or unit. However, it is essential that any team's players be afforded an opportunity to interact in the training seminar or classroom. This will create positive group dynamics for the later challenges.

Teambuilding Ills

EMPHASIZE TEAMBUILDING AND problem-solving techniques, not cultures. Teambuilding is not imported from Japan or anywhere else. Teamwork is as uniquely and fundamentally American as any management principle. Unfortunately, Japanese and other nations' quality and productivity strides suggest that teams were "not invented here," but somewhere across the sea. Teamwork is implicit in almost every American endeavor. What American organizations may lack is the cohesion necessary for planning a long-term strategy and focusing the team's efforts toward a common goal.

The Japanese have contributed substantially to problem-solving, including cause-and-effect analysis (the Ishikawa "fishboning"), design of experiments (Taguchi methods), and the still-viable Quality Circles (in Japan). What teams must learn, though, is that effective problem-solving techniques have no nationality. All successes in their application are fleeting, unless there is commitment to continuous improvement.

Recognize the diversity of teams. A team must be developed, coached, and counseled based on its composition, background, and experience. Teams may have substantially different mixes of employee tenure, job skills, ethnicity, and personality. Teams need training and on-the-job direction based on an assessment of what new resources are needed for team members to become a viable team unit.

Unfortunately, some standardized training programs and TQ resources address groups of people as common commodities. They leave little room for teaching "soft" people skills, such as listening, group dynamics, and conflict resolution. Each group of individuals needs training and coaching. The TQM visionary must not build an initiative wherein all team members must accrue pre-determined training hours, or complete a certain number of "modules."

Teamwork must be established over time. There is no prescribed period

151

within which teams and individuals can acquire all the credentials to be successful. The TQ process involves committing substantial resources for the long term with no definitive milestone for reward or payback. A successful team is built on knowledge, respect and coaching. There must also be an integral need to use the creative resources of all contributors for the overall good of the enterprise. The firm's management must understand and accept that payback in the current fiscal year will not happen and that efficiency or productivity increases are not even a stated objective of the process.

Teambuilding is not teamwork. Because the company is teambuilding, the result may not be teamwork. Organization, planning, training, and all the activities associated with starting the initiative are part of the team development process. These activities, in themselves, do not mean that teamwork has occurred.

Teams are not social clubs. The end result of training and maturation is a functioning company unit with consummate problem-solving skills. The training process is designed to provide and develop certain skills. If team members can provide no more feedback from teambuilding than "we got to know each other better," or "we communicate better," then the process still has further to go. Social interaction is important, but it is only part of the task. Frequent, enjoyable, and fun meetings are good; definitive progress toward work-related goals is paramount. The TQ steering committee must assure that the program doesn't become a series of social engagements, with no focus on prime objectives.

Teams must be synchronized with the organization. Teams and their individual contributors must abide by the fundamental rules, policies, and procedures that guide the company's daily business operations. Teams, leaders, and facilitators are given great latitude in applying their team-building and training experiences. However, they should not have open-ended authority that transgresses normal and prudent operating rules.

While assertiveness and innovation should be encouraged, individual teams cannot be given a "blank check" for operating in opposition to any company guideline. Teams must continue to relate to other individuals, teams, departments, and work groups as equals in a common enterprise and without any perceived superiority.

Teams must be held accountable for their actions. In a true team environment, groups are given appropriate authority and then held responsible for outcomes, just like executives, managers, and supervisors in the business. The goal-setting process is an important building block because it not only focuses team efforts, but also provides a benchmark for success. If goals are not accomplished or the team's actions are consistently ill-timed, the team planning process must be reviewed. People, individually and collectively, must be held accountable for the bottom-line outcomes of team action. In a mature, well-functioning team, the leader and facilitator collectively address team accountability as a vital and constant issue. If a team does not readily accept accountability for work goals, then additional training, coaching, or team leader assessment may be necessary.

Teams cannot operate in a vacuum. Supervisors and managers must be constantly aware of team agendas, actions, and project status. They should meet with facilitators if goals or milestone accomplishments are in doubt. The organization must never assume that a team is totally independent of the main organization's management or technical resources.

Some Team Failure Symptoms

No matter how great an effort or resource expenditure, even the most visionary company can face instances where teams will simply not meld adequately. Depending on the situation, the team may require dissolution and reformation, permanent disbanding, or some other treatment. The following list describes conditions that signal team failure. Note that all teams, like people, will have unproductive days; the team leader and facilitator must, however, discern and distinguish a "bad day" from a trend.

Lack of spirited discussion and disagreement. If there are little or no disagreements in team meetings, it may mean that team members are holding back their true feelings and opinions. This symptom might also be called conspicuous conformity, or "not rocking the boat." Communications within the group are cautious and guarded, and information is not shared. In a good team environment, individuals are not afraid to voice their opinions, or disagree honestly.

Using formal communications and salutations. There are times when a team must communicate by means other than casual conversation. When casual conversation or information is suddenly formalized, however, concern for the recipient's reaction comes into play. The writer may feel a need to establish barriers, using formal salutations like "Mr." and "Ms.": to chill relationships. Written communication also may indicate fear of a face-to-face encounter with the recipient.

Increased use of criticism. If criticism and verbal innuendo become the norm for group operation, there will be little progress. Further, if the actions a team leader takes are based on critical opinions, team cohesion will suffer, and consensus on any action or direction may be difficult.

Lack of progress in team meetings and activities. Meetings are excellent indicators of a team's success. Poor meetings signal a need for the team facilitator and steering committee to assess team issues and perhaps intervene. Poor meetings are characterized by unclear or missing agendas, bored participants, unnecessary length, lack of consensus on simple issues, bickering, and domination by one or a few members. Listen to post-meeting commentary; if the comments include phrases like "I'm glad that's over," or "Now we can get back to our real work," success is doubtful.

Sometimes teams are overly optimistic when scheduling or setting goals. If goals are unrealistic, conflict may arise or there may be little commitment to them. Each member of the team should agree on the group's objectives. If the group agrees that unrealistic goals have been set, the team facilitator should step in to help reassess the situation.

Failure to use available resources. Again, this is a situation for the team facilitator and the team leader. Ineffective teams are often unaware of the true resources and diversity "brought to the table" by its members. As a result, the group's skills and talents are under-utilized. Occasionally, more senior or experienced team members will wait for a mistake, then use the opportunity to say "I told you so," or "I knew that was going to happen, but nobody asked me." From the very first meeting, the team must be encouraged to use its innate creative resources to attack what members agree are prime issues.

Team conversations should normally emphasize "we" and "us," rather than "I." When team members begin actively competing for "air-time" to brag about their personal accomplishments, the team is in trouble. The team leader should take time to review and reinforce the principles that distinguish teams from other work groups. Team accomplishments, not self-aggrandizement, are paramount.

CHAPTER 16

Self–Direction and Empowerment

"It's ours now. Let's work smarter."

– A Trans World Airlines employee

MANY CLAIM THAT THE TEAMS of the future will be totally self-directed or empowered. Whether this comes to pass depends on how business owners and their employees accept the many duties and responsibilities that come with self-direction. Self-direction and empowerment are unique and powerful, but only in the hands of enlightened and responsible individuals.

Just because a business starts a team initiative does not mean it is predisposed to empowerment. Self-direction and empowerment are effective only when two parties, labor and management, are willing and able to assume the inherent responsibilities. A "30-day, money-back" trial period is impossible. Furthermore, managers and supervisors must be willing to collapse their spans of control, and grant authority to others.

Empowerment

LITERALLY, EMPOWERMENT MEANS the giving of power. The prefix, *em-*, means to put on or cover with, and power means dominion, control, or authority. Empowerment then can be said to mean passing control or authority from one group to another; in this case, from the management of a business to its employees.

A business empowers its employees when it allows them to assume greater and greater job responsibilities, and exercise the accumulated job knowledge they possess. In the case of managers and executives, the empowerment process is generally constant. Individuals grow in managerial skill and hone their proficiency in directing people and tasks. At a lower level, however, the empowerment process is much slower, if it exists at all.

It has been difficult for American managers to deal with employee empowerment for several reasons. Many of these reasons relate to job assignments, structure, procedural and labor management issues, and some degree of "historical inertia." In many cases, factory or office worker tasks are so stratified and simplified that there seems to be little opportunity for additional productivity or quality improvement. In other cases, the job has been described in great detail and procedurally "set in stone" bargaining agreements.

Also, some employees are simply not ready or willing to accept the additional job responsibilities that coexist with empowerment. It is sometimes frightening and difficult for an individual to accept a new authority vista when he or she has always been managed by others.

Empowerment is a classic example of a two-edged sword. Management and labor both must be enlightened and trained. Both also must expect a great deal of anxiety when an initiative is implemented.

The Self-Directed Team

IN A TQ SCENARIO, EMPOWERED WORK GROUPS or teams may become self-directed. Theoretically, this means that employee talents are being used creatively and to their fullest potential. A self-directed team (SDT) is an intact group of employees normally responsible for a work process, department, segment, or operation cell. The group is responsible for delivering a product or service to an internal or external customer, monitoring the production process, and taking appropriate actions to assure consistency in quality and productivity. Collectively, the group is responsible for managing the production process and themselves.

By definition, an SDT cannot be a group loosely brought together for a specific task or project. Work is assigned to an SDT in segments discrete enough to give the team ownership. In manufacturing, an SDT might be assigned an entire contiguous assembly line that produces a given product or sub-assembly. In a service industry, the SDT might be responsible for a single core function, such as controlling and distributing packages for overnight delivery to a specific geographic zone.

Self-directed teams are distinguished by several characteristics:

- they design, plan, monitor, and improve the work processes within their area of responsibility. This is not to say they do not or cannot recruit outside resources as appropriate;
- they monitor and inspect their work, taking appropriate actions to correct deficiencies. The SDT is collectively responsible for quality problems;
- they coordinate with other departments and company functions;
- they deal with suppliers and vendors, including those other departments and individuals in the firm that supply them as "internal customers";
- they create and monitor their own schedules, staffing assignments, and performance indicators. They report performance and progress to business unit management;
- they perform certain select managerial and leadership functions within established guidelines or control limits. Generally, they are given the authority needed to carry out the special work unit's everyday tasks;
- they create and monitor their own budgets; and they plan and implement training programs or materials appropriate to the unit's tasks and level of expertise.

A review of these characteristics makes it clear that implementing a self-directed team concept should not be taken lightly, either by management or otherwise highly successful TQ teams.

Readiness for Empowerment and SDTs

THERE ARE NO RELIABLE FORMULAS that address whether an organization is ready to undertake the transition to empowered and self-directed teams. Much of the answer lies in the degree of success simple teams and teamwork have had and the degree to which a continuous improvement philosophy has been achieved. The following list may be helpful.

Organizational readiness means:

- managers are willing to allow responsibility to drift downward in the organization;

- management understands that empowerment and SDTs demand time, patience, and significant allocation of resources;
- management earnestly believes that employees are capable of making critical business decisions;
- the local bargaining unit is willing to re-negotiate work rules and job classifications for greater work group flexibility;
- product, schedule, and technology considerations create more flexibility in running the business;
- the stability of business allows for continuing job and employment stability while the empowerment process matures;
- work may be organized so that entire job or functional responsibility may be assigned to specific teams; and
- management understands that the basic manner in which business is conducted will change forever.

Team readiness means:

- TQ teams have been implemented, are mature, and are realizing payback;
- the nature of work supports a team-based, rather than individual, work environment;
- team training programs in human relations and technical topics have yielded positive results in application;
- team members can absorb additional assignments;
- teams have the technical skills to recognize problems and to request aid from outside resources; and
- team members are curious, concerned, and generally enthusiastic about the empowerment process.

If the conditions listed for organizational and team readiness are not found in your organization, you must forget empowerment until they are.

Poor implementation of self-directed teams can destroy years of effort spent founding new teamwork and continuous improvement concepts. In the United States, the concept of teamwork is not new. True empowerment of teams is. Advance cautiously.

INDEX

ABOUT THE AUTHOR

GENE MILAS is an industrial engineering and quality management consultant, and the principal of a consulting firm founded in 1983. He has consulting, training, and facilitation experience in the automotive, electronics, aircraft, aerospace, and building materials industries. Prior to entering the consulting field, he worked in industry for several years in manufacturing, industrial engineering, and production management. Milas holds BS and MBA degrees and is active in several professional societies, including the Institute of Industrial Engineers (IIE) and the American Society for Quality Control (ASQC). He lives in Tampa, Florida.

About EMP

ENGINEERING & MANAGEMENT PRESS (EMP) is the award-winning book publishing division of the Institute of Industrial Engineers (IIE). EMP was awarded the 1996 *Association Trends* Publishing Award for best book/manual in the soft cover category for *Manufacturing and the Internet* by Richard Mathieu. EMP was also one of four finalists for the 1996 Literary Marketplace *Corporate Achievement Award* in the Professional Category.

EMP was founded in 1981 as Industrial Engineering & Management Press (IE&MP). In 1995, IE&MP was reengineered as Engineering & Management Press. As both IE&MP and EMP, the press has a history of publishing successful titles, such as *Toyota Production Systems, Winning Manufacturing, Managing Quality in America's Most Admired Companies,* and *Beyond the Basics of Reengineering.*

Persons interested in submitting manuscripts to the press should contact Forsyth Alexander, Book Editor, EMP, 25 Technology Park, Norcross, GA 30092.

ABOUT IIE

FOUNDED IN 1948, THE INSTITUTE of Industrial Engineers (IIE) is comprised of more than 25,000 members throughout the United States and 89 other countries. IIE is the only international, nonprofit professional society dedicated to advancing the technical and managerial excellence of industrial engineers and all individuals involved in improving overall quality and productivity. IIE is committed to providing timely information about the profession to its membership, to professionals who practice industrial engineering skills, and to the general public.

IIE provides continuing education opportunities to members to keep them current on the latest technologies and systems that contribute to career advancement. The Institute provides products and services to aid in this endeavor, including professional magazines, journals, books, conferences, and seminars. IIE is constantly working to be the best available resource for information about the industrial engineering profession.

For more information about membership in IIE, please contact IIE Member and Customer Service at 800-494-0460 or 770-449-0460 or cs.@www.iienet.org.

INDUSTRIAL MANAGEMENT

FOR NEARLY 40 YEARS, *Industrial Management* magazine has been serving the needs of business managers concerned with improving processes, productivity, and quality. In every industry–from manufacturing to service to government, *Industrial Management* provides in-depth and insightful coverage of topics like these:

business process reengineering, collective bargaining, concurrent engineering, cycle time reduction, forecasting, human resources strategies, industrial organization, Kaizen, Kanban material acquisition, labor relations, maintenance, management of technology, manufacturing management, operations improvement, organizational behavior, performance measurement, planning, production, productivity, quality, rapid prototyping, scheduling, service, strategic planning, theory of constraints, total quality management, union relations, and work teams.

Every other month, *Industrial Management* provides case studies, practical advice, and hands-on techniques. Subscribers learn from the experiences of others how to avoid unnecessary and potentially costly mistakes–and keep their careers in management on the right track. Each issue contains articles that present to readers both the how and the why of management techniques before they try them out in the workplace.

Industrial Management, a bimonthly magazine, is the official publication of the Society for Engineering and Management Systems (SEMS) of the Institute of Industrial Engineers (IIE). Current subscription rates: $39.00 per year (within the United States); $50.00 per year (outside the U.S.). Prices are subject to change. Discounts are available to members of IIE. There is an additional charge for airmail delivery. To subscribe or to receive more information, contact IIE Member and Customer Service at 800-494-0460 or 770-449-0460 or visit our web site at www.iienet.org.

OTHER BOOKS FROM EMP

TEAMBUILDING AND
TOTAL QUALITY
A Guidebook To TQM Success
by GENE MILAS
hardcover, 1997
ISBN 0-89806-173-3
order code: MILTQM
list price $29.95

LESSONS TO BE LEARNED
JUST IN TIME
by JAMES J. CAMMARANO
hardcover, 1997
ISBN 0-89806-162-7
order code: LESSON
list price $34.95

SIMULATION MADE EASY
A Manager's Guide
by CHARLES HARRELL, PH.D.,
and KERIM TUMAY
311 pages, hardcover, 1995
ISBN 0-89806-136-9
order code: SIMSFY
list price $50.00

FACILITIES AND
WORKPLACE DESIGN
An Illustrated Guide
by QUARTERMAN LEE with ARILD ENG
AMUNDSEN, WILLIAM NELSON, and
HERBERT TUTTLE
232 pages, softcover, 1997
ISBN 0-89806-166-0
order code: FACDGN
list price $25.00

DESIGN OF EXPERIMENTS FOR PROCESS
IMPROVEMENT
AND QUALITY ASSURANCE
by ROBERT F. BREWER, P.E.
280 pages, softcover, 1996
ISBN 0-89806-165-2
order code: BREWER   list price $25.00

ESSENTIAL CAREER SKILLS
FOR ENGINEERS
by SHAHAB SAEED, P.E.,
and KEITH JOHNSON, P.E.
112 pages, softcover, 1995
ISBN 0-89806-142-3
order code: BUSSKI list price $25.00

WORK SIMPLIFICATION
An Analyst's Handbook
by PIERRE THÉRIAULT
200 pages, hardcover, 1996
ISBN 0-89806-163-6
order code: THERIA list price $25.00

BY WHAT METHOD?
by D. SCOTT SINK, PH.D.,
and WILLIAM T. MORRIS, P.E.
364 pages, softcover, 1995
ISBN 0-89806-141-5
order code: BWM752 list price $30.00

TOYOTA PRODUCTION SYSTEM
An Integrated Approach to Just-In-Time
by YASUHIRO MONDEN, PH.D.
425 pages, hardcover, 1993
ISBN 0-89806-129-6
order code: NWTYPS list price $53.95

To order books from EMP

or to request a free catalog of EMP's titles, please call IIE Member
& Customer Service at 800-494-0460 or 770-449-0460. We also
invite you to visit us on IIE's web site at http://www.iienet.org.